YALE STUDIES IN ATTITUDE AND COMMUNICATION

Volume 4

EDITED BY CARL I. HOVLAND

YALE STUDIES IN ATTITUDE AND COMMUNICATION

Social Judgment

ASSIMILATION AND CONTRAST EFFECTS
IN COMMUNICATION AND ATTITUDE CHANGE

by Muzafer Sherif and Carl I. Hovland

New Haven and London
Yale University Press, 1961

Copyright © 1961 by Yale University.
Set in Baskerville type and
printed in the United States of America by
Vail-Ballou Press, Inc., Binghamton, N.Y.
All rights reserved. This book may not be
reproduced, in whole or in part, in any form
(except by reviewers for the public press),
without written permission from the publishers.
Library of Congress catalog card number: 61-14432
Publication of this volume was aided by
the Louis Stern Memorial Fund.

PREFACE

WRITING THIS PREFACE is a lonely task. This book, like the previous three volumes in the series, is a tribute to Carl I. Hovland's life work. On April 16, 1961, the Yale Communication and Attitude Change Program and the Studies in Attitude and Communication lost their founder, and the entire research area probably its most resourceful, persistent, and ingenious experimentalist. The growth of the present volume since the late 1940's is itself a testimony to Carl's particular qualities of scientific caution, enduring concentration, and resourceful devotion to exploration of an important problem area in human affairs.

Having contributed during World War II to research under military auspices on communication and attitude assessment, Carl Hovland returned to his academic setting with a fuller realization of the complexity of factors and of the inadequacy of closed or oversimplified models. Thus, in his research program at Yale, he encouraged theoretical and experimental exploration of a wide variety of current approaches to attitudes and communication, as reflected in the volumes of this series.

In 1948, we discussed the feasibility of a research approach to attitudes and attitude change in terms of basic findings and principles from laboratory studies of judgment in general and of assimilation-contrast effects in particular. Hovland pointed to gaps then existing and urged that solid evidence and further experimental grounds be secured. With his characteristic scientific caution, he preferred that the gaps be filled before formulation of the approach be undertaken. At that time, it seemed that formulation of the assimilation-contrast approach developed in this volume would have to wait until certain prerequisite steps were taken.

First, the judgment effects on which this approach could be based were mainly found in experiments utilizing motivationally neutral stimuli. If principles underlying these effects were to be utilized, specific accommodation had to be made for motivational factors, including ego-involvement. The most elaborated procedures for scaling attitudes at the time (Thurstone scaling) were based on the assumption of independence of the categorization process from attitude or ego-involvement of the individual judge.

Second, and closely related to the first, there was a gap between survey-type studies of attitudes and the then flourishing research on effects of attitudes and other motivational factors in social judgment and perception. An attempt had to be made to pull them together.

Third, in the judgment literature, contrast effects were considered to be established, but, on the whole, assimilation effects either were ignored or, when noted, were often referred to by some such label as the "reverse of contrast."

Almost a decade was devoted to our collaborative efforts to take care of the above mentioned considerations. These efforts started while I was associated with Carl Hovland's program at Yale and, after 1949, continued with aid of supporting grants from the Yale Communication and Attitude Change Program to the University of Oklahoma. The first step, in 1948, was an exploratory study undertaken with Edmund Volkart to assess attitudes in terms of latitudes of acceptance and rejection on the "closed shop" issue, with members of the Yale Political Union serving as subjects. Encouraged by the trends obtained, we initiated other research units with associates and assistants whose contributions are noted in the published results or in the acknowledgments following this preface.

The next research unit was an investigation of judgment of verbal items concerning the social position of Negroes. This research enabled us to specify the attributes of stimuli and procedures conducive, on the one hand, to displacement as a function of the individual's attitude and, on the other, to placement independent of attitude. The characteristic distributions of judgments by individuals with differing attitudes warranted the introduction of the concepts of *raised threshold of acceptance* and *lowered threshold of rejection*. These concepts were also inferred from the constricted or extended widths of the individual's *own categories* for acceptance and rejection as a function of his attitudes on social issues (Chapter 5). The demonstrated relationships provided a functional basis for understanding the constricted latitude of acceptance of individuals who are strongly involved in their stands on an issue and the more extensive latitude of acceptance of individuals less deeply concerned with the issue.

It was a logical next step to demonstrate that reactions to communication, as well as susceptibility or resistance to change, by individuals confronted with a specific communication on a social issue are related to the discrepancy between characteristic latitudes of acceptance and the position advocated in the communication. Our researches utilized the controversial issues of prohibition in the then "dry" Oklahoma and the 1956 presidential election campaign. More recently, because of a few puzzling problems on assimilation effects in these studies, upon Carl Hovland's urging, a more extensive investigation was initiated in the Pacific Northwest and the Southwest prior to the 1960 presidential election, with a grant from the Rockefeller Foundation.

Our efforts to relate findings from the psychophysical laboratory to the study of social judgment are presented in Chapters 2–4. Because assimilation and contrast effects were basic in the approach, a psychophysical study was carried out in the mid-fifties, with the collaboration of Daniel Taub, B. Jack White, and William Robert Hood, which established assimilation as well as contrast effects as a function of differing anchor stimuli (Chapter 3). With the support of Carl Hovland's program, O. J. Harvey of the University of Colorado and Donald T. Campbell of Northwestern University demonstrated differential effects of anchors with narrow and wide stimulus ranges and varying amounts of practice.

The research mentioned briefly here and the related studies made during the last ten years and reported in the text were essential to the conception of the present volume. The development of the present research approach is a specific instance of the way Carl Hovland assiduously pursued conceptual and methodological threads despite tremendous pressures on his time from his multifaceted program and continuing demands for consultation in research matters from various foundations and agencies. For those who knew him, Carl Hovland's dedication of his keen mind set him apart as a scholar hard to match in academic and research circles. The example of his modesty and intellectual integrity, his searching mind, and dedicated life in research will be sorely missed by all who work in this and related areas.

The several revisions of the manuscript had the benefit in whole or in part of the constructive reactions of various colleagues, among whom we are especially grateful to Irving L. Janis and Fred D. Sheffield of Yale University, Clarence H. Graham of Columbia University, Dwight W. Chapman of Vassar College, Gardner Murphy of the Menninger Foundation, and Claire Selltiz of New York University. However, in no way are they responsible for the organization and content of the final manuscript. We are indebted to Robert Abelson of Yale in matters of statistical analysis and presentation.

Association with John Volkmann of Mt. Holyoke College, whose research and that of his associates was indispensable in formulating the approach, has been invaluable in tying basic principles of judgment to problems of attitude and attitude change. The works of Harry Helson of the University of Texas, which constitute a milestone in insisting on the wide implications of the psychology of judgment, and later personal association with him have been a great source of support in maintaining our efforts. For preparation of materials, writing portions of various chapters in the first draft, for work in the several revisions of the manuscript, and especially the final revision in the fall of 1960, Carolyn W. Sherif contributed substantially.

The appearance of this volume owes much to Jane Olson of the Yale University Press for perceptive editorial work and effective coordination in publishing this volume. A special debt is due to Jane Olejarczyk for typing parts of the several revisions and preparing the reference list, as well as ever-ready help in attending to various tasks. Thanks are extended to Dorothy Kendall of Norman, Oklahoma, for typing the first draft of the manuscript and Barbara Hulett of Seattle, Washington, for typing most of the final revision.

The volume as well as the collaborative research units reported in it was made possible through grants by the Rockefeller Foundation to Carl Hovland's research program. The support of the Foundation and the keen interest of Leland C. DeVinney are gratefully acknowledged.

The time for my concentration on writing and research has been made available through the policy of President George L. Cross of the University of Oklahoma which accentuates research on attitudes and human groups as an indispensable part of the university functions. I extend my thanks to Pete Kyle McCarter and Lloyd E. Swearingen, whose administrative judgment greatly facilitated the arrangements.

MUZAFER SHERIF

Norman, Oklahoma
August, 1961

RESEARCH ACKNOWLEDGMENTS

IN ADDITION TO those individuals and institutions mentioned in the Preface, the contributions of others in specific ways are gratefully acknowledged below or in published reports included in the reference list of this book.

Several persons collaborated in research, supported in part by the Yale Communication and Attitude Change Program, which is reported in publication for the first time here. These include William Robert Hood, now of Texas College of Arts and Industries, who participated in the study on judgment and verbal report (Chapter 4) and Lawrence La Fave, now Research Analyst with the Cook County Welfare Agency, who collaborated in the study on judgment of the segregation issue (Chapter 5). In preparation of the communications, securing subjects, administration of procedures, or tabulation and analysis of data, the following persons collaborated in the study of the 1956 election campaign (Chapters 6 and 7): Henry Pronko, University of Wichita; Robert Scofield, State University of Oklahoma; Jack Douglas, University of Oklahoma; and W. R. Hood, Lawrence La Fave, George Rucker, Lee Thayer, Robert Killian, and William LeFurgy —all of the University of Oklahoma at the time.

The following persons generously made their unpublished research available for our use: James O. Whittaker, now of Gustavus Adolphus College (Chapter 3); B. Jack White, now of the University of Utah (Chapter 3); S. I. Perlo of Yale University (Chapter 4); Bernard Mausner of the University of Pittsburgh (Chapter 5); Melvin Manis of the University of Michigan (Chapter 7); and W. R. Hood (Chapter 8).

Lawrence La Fave assisted through surveys of experimental literature on attitude and attitude change, and Nicholas Pollis surveyed the differing evaluations of Supreme Court Justices (Chapter 1).

M.S.

CONTENTS

Judgmental Processes
and Problems of Attitude

THE PRESENT VOLUME, like previous ones in this series, is concerned with basic psychological processes underlying the expression of attitudes and their modifiability through communication. Attitude measurement, whether the indices are overt behavior or, more typically, check marks on an attitude questionnaire, is based upon evaluations and categorization of the stimuli toward which the attitude is held. Thus stimulus conditions, internalized anchors, motivation, prior learning, and a host of other factors affect the response obtained in the measurement. These factors are of course also involved when attitudes are changed through communication. It is fortunate that there is a considerable body of research on how these factors affect judgment of simpler stimulus material under well-controlled laboratory conditions. The present volume examines these studies to obtain leads as to factors which will be relevant for the more complex problems of social attitudes and attitude change. On the basis of generalizations derived from analyses of the basic judgmental process an attempt is made to describe attitudes and attitude change through communication in terms which are consonant with those utilized in describing judgmental processes. It is hoped in this way to effect a closer rapprochement between these two hitherto diverse fields of investigation.

In order to demonstrate judgment processes and principles in the clearest form, the early chapters present illustrative studies on judgment of relatively simple and motivationally neutral stimulus material. They may serve as a baseline. Nevertheless, accommodation is made for motivational and other factors. Operation of the judgment principles in relation to factors of motivation and learning is then discussed. The generalizations thus reached and the hunches they generate are then applied to problems of attitude and attitude change.

TRADITIONAL APPROACHES TO ATTITUDE AND ATTITUDE CHANGE

Studies of attitude conducted during the twenties and thirties were mainly of the "survey" type in which individuals were asked to check prepared categories on an issue. The primary concern was with the extent to which different groups held particular attitudes, for example the difference between attitudes toward war of student and nonstudent populations. Relatively little concern was manifested in regard to the psychological processes underlying the individual's expression of his attitudes or to the pattern of stimulus conditions under which the responses were obtained. Thurstone (1929) and his associates made a major contribution in providing more systematic means for scaling attitudinal responses. But their underlying assumption, that the intervals between various positions on an attitude scale are independent of the position of the individual who is making the judgments, has been called into question by the research of the writers (Hovland and Sherif, 1952; Sherif and Hovland, 1953). It now appears that distances between different points on an attitude scale derived by the method of equal-appearing intervals are affected by the position of the individual making the evaluation (cf. Chap. 5).*

During the same span of years interest in the effect of communications on attitudes was largely in showing that changes in questionnaire or "attitude scale" checkings occur as a consequence of exposure to communication. There was much less concern with the psychological processes underlying the changes. Considerable divergence in results was obtained, some showing change in the direction of the communication and others showing shifts in the opposite direction. Thus while a number of studies showed that lecturers, pamphlets, and motion pictures could produce changes in attitude, few studies were made until the forties to show how specific content transmitted by specific communicators affects particular audiences (cf. e.g. Hovland, Lumsdaine, and Sheffield, 1949).

The change which has taken place in the analysis of attitudes is well illustrated by the studies presented in the recent special issue of the *Public Opinion Quarterly* (Katz, ed., 1960). It will be seen that in the fifties there has been an increased concern with fundamental factors underlying attitudes and their modification. Illustrative of recent approaches to these problems are the studies of Heider (1958) and Festinger (1957). It is the writers' belief, however, that attitude research should be more solidly based on previous work in basic psychological processes, particularly of judgment. What appears to be seriously needed is more extensive exploration of the underlying principles governing attitudinal evaluations by the individual and the factors by which such evaluations are modified. It is to this type of analysis that the present volume is addressed.

* We are not challenging the general usefulness of Thurstone scaling procedures, since under most circumstances the degree of personal involvement and bias of judges and of subjects whose attitudes are being evaluated is much less than that invoked in our studies. But our results do indicate that "equal

RELEVANCE OF JUDGMENT PROCESSES TO ATTITUDE PROBLEMS

In the most recent volume of this series the organization of attitudes was considered by analyzing the interrelationship between cognitive, affective, and behavioral components of attitudes. In the present volume we probe even more deeply into one phase of this process, the cognitive aspect, to consider how the individual views the issue and the way his judgments are shaped by external and internal factors. Our underlying assumption is that the processes of judgment are critical for understanding research findings in the area of attitude and attitude change. A few illustrations may serve to give substance to our assumption.

During the baseball season, one may observe judgments from thousands of spectators relative to the decisions of the umpire. When he declares the verdict "You're out" against their favored team, the boos from the partisans are resounding expressions of their own judgment of the event. Of course, the fans are capable of making objectively correct judgments if they have the opportunity to examine all the details of the episode through slow-motion pictures. However, in complex stimulus situations such as that in a crowded stadium, "committed" individuals with a strong attitude on an issue do not wait: they readily *pass judgments* and *act* in terms of them.

As the above example implies, a person's attitude on an issue may well influence the way he appraises relevant behavior and events. Thus individuals who straddle the fence in public life are frequently judged differently by people holding one extreme position than by people taking an extreme stand on the opposite side. For example, the vacillating labor leader, Samuel Gompers, was judged as rather radical

intervals" are often not actually equal subjectively, as Thurstone hoped they would be.

by the conservatives of his day, but he was dubbed a conservative by left-wingers in the labor movement. Supreme Court justices Charles Evans Hughes and (probably to a lesser extent) Owen J. Roberts balanced between the "conservatives" and "liberals" of the "Roosevelt court" in the thirties. Evaluations rendered by various authors of these two justices are strongly colored by the attitudes of the writer passing judgment. Liberal writers tend to place these justices on the conservative side, but this is not the judgment of writers who are not liberals.

As discussed in earlier volumes of this series, an attitude toward an object, person, group, or social issue is not directly observable but is inferred from a persistent and *characteristic* mode of reaction to that stimulus or stimulus class. This characteristic mode of reaction signifies differential treatment of the object of attitude. It is inferred that the object of attitude is placed in a category or class favorable or unfavorable in some degree, high or low in some degree, acceptable or unacceptable in some degree in the individual's scheme of things. In short, one essential aspect of the attitudinal reaction is a categorization process, whether or not the individual is aware that he is passing a judgment.

Categorization As an Essential Aspect of Attitudinal Response

When one solicits an expression of an individual's attitude toward some social issue, person, or group, one typically finds that the process involves placement of the issue in a framework and assignment to a category. Thus if a person (who is a practicing member of one of the religious groups that use some kind of baptism as part of the initiation of new members) is asked to express his attitude toward baptism, he is likely to place baptismal ceremonies into differentiated rankings, the preferred practice of his own group probably being

at the top and serving as the standard. Likewise, if one asks
an individual for his opinion as to acceptability of various
groups, he is likely to place them in a certain number of
categories ranging from encouragement of close personal association, through the category of tolerating residence in his
own neighborhood, all the way to the category of desiring
their exclusion from the country. We typically find that the
individual has internalized categories designating relative
positions or "social distance" for placement of the individual
in a group, and that each category is endowed with certain
qualities. A person's attitude is revealed in his favorable or
derogatory reactions regulated by the category in question
and by the attributes attached to that category. If the X
group is "endowed" by the Y group with qualities a, b, and c
(favorable or unfavorable) the representative members of the
Y group will tend to see these qualities in the collective or
individual behavior of the X group and react accordingly in
a characteristic way.

DIFFERENTIATION OF JUDGMENT PROCESSES: DISCRIMINATION, PLACEMENT, AND ACCEPTANCE-REJECTION

From the point of view of conceptual analysis and experimental specification, it is feasible to differentiate the judgment process in various ways. A conceptual differentiation
can be made in terms of item discrimination, placement of
items, and acceptance-rejection of items. A great deal of experimental work has accumulated along each of these three
lines.

Discrimination refers to the task of identifying a stimulus
item (a weight, a tone, a statement) as different from another
item. The tremendous amount of work dealing with just
noticeable differences (j.n.d.s) between two stimuli differing
along the same dimension is representative. Some relevant

aspects of this research are touched upon in Chapter 2, but most of this research has little bearing on our problem.

It is convenient to refer to that kind of discrimination which locates a given stimulus relative to more than two other discriminable items as *placement* or *categorization* of the item. Studies dealing with scaling of neutral items, like weights or tones, are representative of this approach. Our concern in this book is primarily with reactions to motivationally relevant items, as exemplified by statements evaluating a social issue or a group of people. However, even in placement of motivationally neutral items, variations occur as a function of the stimulus arrangements and procedures of the experimental conditions. Therefore, if the effects of attitudes upon placement of items are to be assessed adequately, it is necessary first to consider judgmental variations attributable to such stimulus arrangements and procedures. In particular, such consideration will yield methodological guides for evaluating the conditions in which attitudinal factors are maximally or minimally effective in producing judgmental variations, such as displacements, over- and under-estimations. The general problem was illustrated earlier with reference to judgments concerning an umpire's verdict at the baseball stadium or on the basis of slow-motion pictures after the game. Problems related to placement will be encountered in Chapters 2, 3, and 4. Chapter 5 will be devoted to a formulation of relationships between attitude and item placement under specified stimulus conditions.

The judgment task carried out under *acceptance-rejection* instructions also requires placement or categorization of items (statements, objects, human groups) in terms of the preferences of the individuals. Scales of judgment instructing the subjects to place the most acceptable items at one end, the most objectionable ones at the other extreme, and other items in appropriate places between the extremes, are representative of this line of analysis. Placement of groups along a social-distance scale and rank-order scales based on preference (such as ranking of composers or painters) are representative of placement in terms of affectively charged attitudes.

In the chapters to follow, especially in Part Two, we shall encounter this kind of categorization in the discussions of the attitude-item placement problem. Chapter 6 will be devoted to our formulation of the relationship between attitude and acceptance-rejection type of placement, and presentation of experimental findings in support of this formulation.

MOTIVATIONAL AND LEARNING FACTORS RELEVANT TO PLACEMENT OF ITEMS

A judgment always involves a comparison between two or more stimuli. For purposes of conceptual analysis, psychologists devise laboratory experiments in which judgment consists of the comparison of only two objects or items. One of the objects is just noticeably heavier, brighter, louder, or longer than the comparison object. Or one stimulus item is noticeably more pleasant or more favorable than another item. The items may be compared simultaneously or successively with a very short interval between presentations. In such experiments, the task is discrimination and the main psychological problem is the keenness of discrimination. When keenness of discrimination (keenness of tactual, visual, auditory, or kinesthetic sense, or keenness in discriminating the dictionary meaning of words) is the principal problem, experimental procedures requiring the subject to make this kind of comparison are suitable.

However, if the primary problem of research concerns the judgmental activity ordinarily involved when a person judges stimuli related to an attitude, the above procedures and analysis may not be appropriate. Procedures suitable for the study of simple discrimination circumscribe the stimulus pattern drastically and thereby constrict the operation of attitudinal factors in the judgment process.

Learning factors. Judgment of a stimulus item relevant to an individual's attitude is necessarily related to other similar items to which the individual has been exposed. The individual forms an attitude as a consequence of repeated encounters with objects, persons, or communications. Comparison of an item related to an attitude is made against a whole background of similar objects which constitutes the range of such objects perceived and categorized on the basis of the individual's prior encounters with them. Therefore, the process of comparison in judgment of a relevant stimulus is not represented by having the individual compare two objects presented simultaneously or in close succession.

We shall refer to the background for a particular comparison as the *reference scale* of the individual in that respect. Placement of stimulus items is made relative to a reference scale formed by the individual. The formation of reference scales by the individual whether in relation to objects, human groups, or social norms is clearly a problem of *learning*. The formation of reference scales is discussed in Chapters 2 and 4.

Motivational factors. As stated above, the judgment of an item relevant to an attitude involves comparison with an appropriate reference scale, rather than a simple comparison between two items as in a typical laboratory experiment on discrimination. It follows that attitudinal judgments are typically of the *placement* type, and this has definite implications for fruitful research practice in this area.

In the study of judgment processes underlying attitudinal reactions, the identification of judgment categories in an individual's reference scale and placement of items within it are crucial problems. For example, in a study of attitudes toward the segregation-desegregation issue, it is necessary to learn what kind and how many categories individuals actually use in judging behavior or verbal statements ranging from the most extreme segregationist position to the most extreme desegregationist position. In assessing an individual's attitude on this issue, it is necessary to know that a person with a desegregationist stand on the issue places statements advocating segregation on the bus or on the train in the unfavorable category. From the outset, research in this area involves the problem of *placement*.

Research on the problem of scaling items relevant to social attitudes has frequently been facilitated by circumscribing the stimuli to be compared in the manner of discrimination experiments. As useful as this procedure may be for test construction, it cannot be regarded as appropriate for studying judgment of items related to attitudes as this activity typically occurs in actual life. The inadequacy of such procedures can be illustrated. Faced with the task of discrimination between the relative favorableness of segregation applied on the train and on the bus, a desegregationist can render a judgment. The fact remains that both examples are in an objectionable category for him. In the discrimination task which requires the individual with a strong attitude on an issue to choose one of two objectionable statements as more favorable than the other, the subject's reactions to such a task and toward the experimenter subjecting him to it may be more significant psychologically than the choice itself.

When the problems of research pertain to the judgmental process underlying specific attitudinal reactions, it is appropriate to use procedures which allow motivational factors to be manifested. If keenness of discrimination is the primary research problem, it is possible, as we have seen, to minimize the effect of attitude or past experience (learning) by circumscribing the judgment situation to the comparison of two clearly defined items and requiring a choice. However, the latter procedure does not represent typical conditions in which the individual judges an attitude-related item. A stimulus related to an attitude is necessarily judged against the reference scale which the individual has formed relative to the particular class of stimulus items in question.

On a scale of positions on a social issue ranging from one extreme to the opposite extreme, for example, one of the positions is appropriated to represent the individual's own stand or commitment. This stand on the issue is a major factor in regulating his relationships with other individuals involving that issue. His acceptances and rejections in that regard are regulated accordingly. As experiments show, placement of items related to the issue is significantly affected by their relative proximity or distance from the individual's own stand. In short, the judgment of items related to an attitude involves placement in terms of the individual's reference scale, but it becomes placement in which the degree of acceptance or rejection is significant.

PSYCHOLOGICAL REFERENCE SCALES AND THE STIMULUS CONDITIONS DURING THEIR FORMATION

Laboratory findings on judgment have shown that placement of a particular stimulus in a series is not made solely in terms of the discrete physical properties of that stimulus. A judgment is rendered in terms of the psychological reference scale which the individual has formed on the basis of his previous encounters with similar stimuli (Chapter 2).

In other words, judgment of a particular stimulus in a series involves placement in categories, and it is influenced by the whole background of similar stimuli which constitutes the basis for an appropriate reference scale. Analysis of the stimulus conditions on the basis of which the individual forms a psychological reference scale has far-reaching implications for the study of judgment of social issues and communication concerning them.

In laboratory studies of judgment, psychological scales are usually formed during repeated presentations of a well-graded series of stimuli (weights, tones, statements). The reference scale consists of categories whose labels are ordinarily provided through instructions. In the traditional experiments, each stimulus to be judged is presented with a *standard* stimulus, which serves as a salient reference point or anchorage in the formation of a psychological scale. However, it was found that the use of a formal standard is not necessary for the formation of a reference scale. If each stimulus is presented singly throughout several presentations of a definite series of stimuli, the individual still forms a scale of judgment consisting of a number of categories. In the latter case, the stimuli at the ends of the particular series are utilized by the individual as anchorages in the formation of a psychological scale (Chapter 2).

Once a psychological scale is formed, subsequent judgment of a similar stimulus is greatly affected by the position of that stimulus relative to the prevailing reference scale. When stimuli are presented with values greater than or less than any in the series which was the basis of the reference scale, the categories of the scale are subject to alterations. These phenomena constitute the area of research investigating reciprocal relationships between psychological scales and anchorages (Chapter 3).

When psychological scales are based on encounters with a well-graded stimulus series such as a definite range of discriminable physical stimuli, there is a close relationship between the stimulus series and the psychological scale. The psychological scale is readily susceptible to adjustments with the addition of new stimuli to the series or with shifts of the total range of the objective stimulus series. This may be one reason why psychological scales related to technological developments in various societies change somewhat more readily than scales related to socio-political and religious values.

Let us go a step further. It is not necessary to have a definitely graded series of stimuli for the formation of psychological scales. Even when the stimulus series is not well graded, individuals still form psychological scales. In these instances, the range of the scale and the number of categories within it are significantly influenced by the judgments of other people. As a result, the stimulus conditions affecting the formation of a reference scale have to include the social setting: established norms, the properties of the interaction among the individuals involved, the general setting of their interaction, the prevailing pattern of relationships among them, and so on.

Once established, psychological scales initially based on *psycho-social actualities* serve a function similar to those based on series of physical gradations. Namely, they serve as a basis for comparison and appraisal of relevant stimulus items on subsequent encounters. Social reference scales that individuals in human groups use in judging political, religious, ethical, and aesthetic matters cannot be gauged against an objectively graded stimulus series. They are psycho-social in origin and can be gauged against social realities. They define and regulate one's relationship to other individuals, groups, social objects, and institutions. A certain category in such a reference scale becomes the individual's preferred category. This position within the scale represents his own stand on the issue and serves as a major anchor in judgment. If the issue is a significant one to him, he is willing to tolerate only slight deviation from this category and finds further deviation obnoxious.

On a social reference scale, we may refer to the range of positions that includes an individual's stand and other positions that he will tolerate as his *latitude of acceptance*. Beyond this, other positions on the issue are rejected, and that range of positions is his *latitude of rejection*. The relationship between the degree of commitment or identification with his own stand and his latitude of acceptance will be investigated in Chapters 5 and 6.

The individual's reactions to a communication and the effect of that communication on his attitude can be studied relative to his established categorizations of the issue, that is, his reference scale for judgment of the issue. Investigation of these problems must determine the location of his latitudes of acceptance and rejection relative to the stand advocated in communication. The resulting information about the individual's placement of the communication and his evaluation of it may clarify problems of attitude change (Chapter 7).

PART ONE

Leads Derived from Studies of Judgment

CHAPTER 2

Stimulus Arrangements and the Formation of Judgment Scales

AN ATTITUDE, as noted in Chapter 1, is inferred from the characteristic pattern of the individual's reactions to a stimulus item. His characteristic pattern of reaction is revealed through some degree of acceptance of or preference for the stimulus item in question. Conversely, it is revealed through rejection or deprecation manifested in varying degrees relative to other stimulus items in the same universe of discourse. All such reactions imply placement or categorization of the attitude-related stimuli and can be ordered along like-dislike or acceptance-rejection dimensions. And categorization is a judgment process.

Categorizations involved in attitude and attitude change may be approached more effectively if pertinent implications from experimental work on judgment are fully explored. One of the notions that emerged from experimental work on judgment which has a direct bearing on attitude studies is the "relativity of judgment." That is, judgment always involves comparison between two or more stimulus items. Differences in the experimentally introduced conditions under which judgment of a stimulus item is rendered produce demonstrable differences in its categorization. For example, it makes a difference whether a stimulus item is categorized relative to another single comparison stimulus or relative to an entire series of stimuli. These two conditions exemplify the topic of stimulus arrangements which we shall discuss in this chapter.

We are interested in the area of judgment primarily for its implications for attitude problems. Yet, keeping an eye on results obtained through methods designed to study keenness of discrimination and categorization is helpful in that they provide baselines for properly evaluating data concerning displacements in categorizations attributable to attitude or attitude change. For this reason, in the next section, we start with a brief discussion of stimulus arrangements where the object of study is keenness of discrimination or categorization, rather than with those where the object of study is the attitude of the individual as inferred from predicted variations in categorizing relevant stimulus items. Then, a brief comparison of a few representative methods in the study of judgment, specifying the stimulus arrangements in each, will provide leads for the choice of particular stimulus arrangements most suited for the study of attitudinal factors through variations in judgment.

In the area of attitude problems, the usual judgmental activity consists of placement of attitude-related items into categories of a judgment scale which the individual has previously formed for that class of items. The psychological scale for judgment of an item, which may be referred to as the individual's reference scale in this regard, is more adequately understood when related to the stimulus conditions in which it was formed. Accordingly we shall characterize briefly certain modal stimulus arrangements in which scales are established.

We shall close the chapter by calling attention to effects of internal anchorages in the placement of items. Experiments on judgment as influenced by internal anchorages have direct bearing for investigation of the ways different individuals react to communications advocating a position on a social issue. More extensive treatment of this topic is reserved for Chapter 4.

STIMULUS ARRANGEMENTS IN MAJOR LINES OF JUDGMENT EXPERIMENTS

In utilizing leads from experiments on judgment, we shall draw on findings from two lines of development which are often considered divergent. These lines of development may be characterized as follows:

1. One line of research stems from the area traditionally called *psychophysics*. Early experimental studies of judgment were concerned mainly with keenness of discrimination and the physiology of receptors. Since the middle of the last century, psychophysical methods have been developed for determining the stimulus values at which, say, a sound becomes discernible (lower threshold), beyond which it ceases to be discernible (terminal threshold), and for determining the ratio of increment necessary for one stimulus to be judged noticeably different from another (difference threshold). Much of the work has involved placement of a series of items into categories provided by the instructions. In the relatively long history of psychophysical work, the emphasis has been on developing methods and procedures that are conducive to accurate judgment, that is, to as close a correspondence as possible between the stimulus object and its placement in the series.

However, psychophysical studies discovered and measured certain "constant errors" of judgment. A constant error consists of a disparity between the "point of subjective equality," which is considered the midpoint of a psychological scale formed in relation to a stimulus series, and the value of a standard stimulus, which is usually around the value of the middle stimulus in a series. In the present discussion, only the most general features of the constant errors which have been studied in traditional psychophysical work are pertinent, but these are significant in any study of judgment.

First, the size and direction of constant errors vary with the procedures and with the stimulus arrangements under which judgment is rendered. For example, especially when no standard is presented for comparison with each stimulus, judgments of stimuli are influenced by the values of preceding stimuli (their magnitude, intensity, and quality, as the case may be). In fact, the order of presentation is routinely varied or counterbalanced in psychophysical research to reduce systematic error attributable to a series effect.

Second, constant errors in traditional psychophysical experiments are, on the whole, deviations from objective stimulus values in the same direction for all individuals rendering judgments under a given experimental condition. In other words, the direction of the constant errors in question is relatively invariant from individual to individual. As Woodworth and Schlosberg (1954, p. 225) point out, such constant errors are of considerable theoretical interest for clarifying the stimulus and organismic factors operative in errors which are not attributable to idiosyncratic factors, social attitudes, or experimentally introduced social factors.

2. *Under given conditions,* which are specified later in this chapter, the judgments of some individuals differ systematically in direction and degree from those made by other individuals. Such variations in judgment are a function of the individual's particular attitude or motive, or of a specific social influence operative in the situation. For example, there are cases in which judgments made by individuals belonging to two different groups are systematically displaced in opposite directions, because of diametrically opposite stands

the two groups uphold concerning the object of judgment (Hovland and Sherif, 1952).

There have been individuals who have shown that they are quite capable of normal discrimination of color shadings in the usual color-matching test, yet whose judgments of the skin shades of other persons were displaced in different directions, depending in part on whether they liked or disliked the person being rated (Marks, 1943). In another experiment, judgments of lines of intermediate length were displaced toward the "longer" direction after subjects had been rewarded for making judgments in the "long" segment of a series (Proshansky and Murphy, 1942).

This second line of development, which is sometimes referred to as a *cognitive* approach, studies systematic variations in judgment as indicators of personality, motivational, or social factors. Research and theory with this emphasis have gained ground since the thirties. Judging or categorizing is one of the cognitive processes. Systematic variations due to a particular attitude, motive, or ego-involvement, or to a social influence introduced by the experimenter have also been found in reactions to given stimulus conditions in the case of other cognitive processes—perceiving (e.g. Gilchrist and Nesberg, 1952; Witkin, 1954), remembering (Bartlett, 1932; Clark, 1940), and imagining (Levine, Chein, and Murphy, 1942; Sanford, 1937).

Demonstrations of systematic errors which differ in direction and degree, owing to the particular individual's attitude, ego-involvement, and/or a social influence, have sometimes led to assertions that we are here dealing with phenomena which transcend judgment and learning (cf. e.g. Bruner, 1946, p. 241; Alper, 1946). Other writers have carried the phenomenology of distortions in judgment and perception to the extent of making judging or perceiving an idiosyncratic affair unique to the private world of each individual. Correctives to such extreme positions, which would almost make judgment or perception of objects independent of objective stimulus checks, have been made by investigators who are interested in the step-by-step analysis of stimulus-judgment relationships and in constant errors that are not peculiar to this or that individual, to this or that group, but are valid in general (Gibson, 1950; Graham, 1958; Volkmann, 1951).

It seems to us that the two apparently divergent approaches briefly characterized above, viz. the psychophysical study of judgment and stimulus relationships on the one hand and the so-called cognitive approach to the study of attitudes, motives, ego-involvements, personality, or social influence through judgment, on the other, need not be antithetical. In fact, through analysis of the research problems, procedures, and stimulus materials typically employed and the responses observed in each, the two developments can benefit each other. In the last analysis, the difference in research strategy amounts to the use of different stimulus conditions, each appropriate for the study of particular problems:

> 1. The study of judgment or perceptual process under well-structured, clearly defined stimulus conditions which minimize or even curtail the operation of attitudinal or social factors.
> 2. The study of attitude, ego-involvement, or social influence through systematic variations in judging or perceiving relevant stimuli along dimensions in which displacements attributable to such variables are facilitated.

The latter of these two research strategies is a major concern in this book. But, in order to gain a sound basis for attributing variations in obtained judgments to attitude, we have to assess the effects of different stimulus arrangements upon errors when the individual's attitude does not become a major factor. If the properties of stimulus arrangements are not considered, we might very well attribute variations in response to attitude when properly they are produced by a particular stimulus arrangement in which the individual makes his judgments. Therefore, we shall briefly indicate the stimulus arrangements typically used in both research developments mentioned above.

If the problem of psychological research concerns keenness of discrimination, the magnitude of sense distances, stimulus determinants of accurate placement, or stimulus correlates of perception, then the appropriate experimental setup is one that (a) uses motivationally neutral material, (b) utilizes a series of stimulus items that is well-defined, and (c) instructs subjects in a way that prevents the fortuitous operation of individual attitudes and of social influence as much as possible.

On the other hand, if our problem concerns the study of attitude or attitude change through systematic variations in cognitive reactions, the stimulus arrangements appropriate in the experimental setup differ from those just summarized. The stimulus material or task is relevant to the attitude being studied. Furthermore, if inferences about attitudes or motives are to be made on the basis of systematic variations in judgment, the stimulus arrangements in which judgment is rendered must permit displacements to occur. The extent of displacement differs from one stimulus arrangement to another. Consequently, if we are to evaluate systematic displacements and attribute them to attitude, some knowledge of the margin for error in the stimulus arrangements is necessary. An appropriate stimulus arrangement for the study of attitude through judgmental variations is one conducive to a substantial margin for displacement.

As the structure of the stimulus dimension to be judged

decreases, as the task becomes more difficult owing to small differences between items, the number of likely alternative reactions becomes greater. Such stimulus arrangements are conducive to greater displacement. But there is a limit to the possible distortion. In any experimental situation, there are at least a few objective conditions which limit response variation. If there were not, systematic errors would not be amenable to experimental study. The more the limits to the magnitude of error and its direction can be specified, the more predictable comparisons will be in terms of the experimental variables.

Whether explicit or not, a basic assumption in investigations of attitude, personality, or social factors through cognitive processes has been as follows: Given appropriate stimulus conditions and procedures, the attitude, motive, or social influence is revealed through systematic errors in the individual's cognitive reactions (judgment, perception, learning, remembering). Thus, every experiment during the last few decades that has demonstrated systematic errors in cognitive processes as a function of attitudes, motives, or personality factors has used procedures and stimulus arrangements conducive to considerable response variation.

The above methodological assumption need not imply, as it is sometimes interpreted, that attitudes, motives, or social influences always operate in the direction of producing error. Instead it is assumed that systematic errors in judgment, under the specified conditions, may indicate the operation of such influences. One advantage of utilizing judgments as response indicators rather than other cognitive reactions (e.g. remembering, imagining) is that judgments are relatively simple and readily obtained in quantitative form in specified dimensions.

The importance of knowing the margin for error in different stimulus arrangements and procedures can best be illustrated by a comparison of a few well-known psychophysical methods which have been rather thoroughly explored.

A Comparison of Methods

A survey of psychophysical methods would take us too far afield from our problem. Comprehensive surveys of psychophysical methods are given in Guilford (1954) and Woodworth and Schlosberg (1954). Here our objective is to compare results obtained by several methods to illustrate how errors in judgment differ according to different stimulus arrangements. The procedures followed in various psychophysical methods present different stimulus arrangements for the individual confronting them, and it has been shown that these varying stimulus arrangements are conducive to differences in results (Edwards, 1957; Stevens, 1951; Woodworth and Schlosberg, 1954).

Stimulus arrangements vary in the definiteness or indefiniteness of the items or objects confronting the individual, their complexity, "numerousness," the manner of presentation in time, the presence or absence of standards or anchorages, the difficulty of the task, and in other ways as well. Here, however, we shall concentrate largely on the manner of presentation and numerousness of the items, as these vary in the paired-comparisons, order-of-merit, and equal-appearing intervals procedures, three of the more frequently used methods in attitude scaling.

Consider first the procedures in each of the three methods and the resulting stimulus arrangements faced by the individual rendering judgments. In paired-comparisons procedures, the subject is confronted on a given trial with only two stimuli simultaneously. His task is to compare the two items by saying which one is "heavier," "greater," "more pleasant," "more favorable," as the case may be. This is ordinarily a rather easy task. By circumscribing the task to two stimuli at a time and instructing the subject to confine himself to discriminating between them, the basis of comparison becomes very clear.

With the order-of-merit procedure, the subject is presented with all the stimulus items at once. Usually, however, the number of items is relatively small, perhaps twenty at most. The subject is told to arrange the items in rank order along some specified dimension. He arranges the items between two extremes and can easily compare items in adjacent ranks if the number is not too large. Thus, the subject ends up by making a series of successive discriminations between adjacent items, rearranging them until he obtains the order he considers correct.

In the equal-appearing intervals procedure, which is used in construction of Thurstone attitude scales, the subject is required to place each stimulus item into a prescribed number of categories which are defined by the experimenter. All of the items are given to him at once, and the number is usually quite large. In fact, the main rationale for this procedure is that it makes possible the securing of judgments for a much larger number of items than by the other methods mentioned. Because of the large number of items, the subject cannot compare each one with every other item and then place them into categories. He actually places them one at a time, perhaps checking back on prior placements; therefore the background of preceding stimuli can easily influence his rating of a particular item.

As one might expect, scale values calculated for a stimulus series judged under the three procedures may differ. Studies by Hevner (1930) and Barrett (1914) have shown, however, that scale values obtained for handwriting specimens on the basis of paired-comparison and order-of-merit procedures are highly correlated when the number of items judged is relatively small (say 15 to 20), and the relationship between them is linear. However, if a large number of items is presented with the order-of-merit procedure, the subject cannot make successive discriminations from item to item with the result that variability, and thus the margin for error, is greater (Conklin and Sutherland, 1923; Hollingworth, 1914).

In the method of equal-appearing intervals, the margin for error is still greater. In Hevner's study (1930) the scale values obtained for handwriting samples by this procedure differed from those calculated from paired comparisons, and the relationship between the two was not linear. Edwards sums up a comparison of the methods of equal-appearing intervals and paired comparisons in a similar way:

> The method of equal-appearing intervals is an absolute scaling method that does not require or force the judges to make fine discriminations. . . . This is not true of the method of paired comparisons where two statements may be close together on the psychological continuum, yet the judge is asked to judge one or the other as being more favorable or more unfavorable as the case may be [Edwards, 1957, p. 113].

To sum up: Stimulus arrangements differ as to the margin for error. Clearly, if the problem of research concerns discriminating ability, the method of study should be one, such as paired comparisons, which allows little room for the intrusion of bases for comparison other than those specifically presented. If, however, the research problem concerns attitudes, with systematic variations in placement as behavioral indicators, then procedures permitting alternative reactions and response variability are appropriate.

Of course, in attitude research, it is often necessary to obtain a rank ordering of items (e.g. statements) for a sample of subjects with as little variance as possible. Procedures which force the individual to make fine discriminations, such as paired comparisons, are highly effective for this limited purpose. However, there are attitude problems which cannot be investigated through such procedures, and one of them is categorization or placement.

In this connection, an observation by Beebe-Center (1932) is pertinent. In an experiment dealing with pleasantness and unpleasantness of stimuli, using the paired-comparisons procedure, one subject gave repeated judgments of "more pleasant" for one stimulus of a pair, yet reported that both of the stimuli were within the "indifference" range for him. On the basis of such observations, Beebe-Center stated that paired-comparison and order-of-merit procedures "yield only relative information—they tell the experimenter nothing concerning the pleasantness, indifference, or unpleasantness of the various stimuli" (p. 35).

In the area of attitude research, the situation is somewhat analogous to asking a Negro subject which is more favorable to the Negro, "to be deprived of a job" or "to be deprived of school facilities in the neighborhood." Probably a discrimination could be made, but it would not reveal that both statements, for him, belong in a category which is highly objectionable.

Now we turn to the psychologically important problem of the formation of judgment scales by the individual. Again we shall be concerned with stimulus arrangements, this time as they affect the formation of judgment scales.

REFERENCE SCALES OF JUDGMENT AND ANCHORAGES

Comparisons are ordinarily made relative to a series of objects or items relevant to the dimension in question. On the basis of encounters with items of a series, the individual forms a psychological scale for judgment consisting of categories applicable to a particular stimulus dimension. Owing to differential experiences with a particular set of stimuli, the judgment scales of different individuals may vary; for example, similar verbal categories may be applied to quite divergent stimulus values.

Thus, a person who has practiced lifting a light series of weights initially judges even the light weights in a new and heavier series as "heavy" (Tresselt, 1947; Wever and Zener, 1928). A profit of $10,000 may be a good one for an individual who has dealt with profits varying, say, between $5,000 and $10,000. The same amount may be judged as "chicken feed" by one who regularly deals with profits exceeding $100,000. Individuals whose prior encounters with a given dimension differ judge the same objects differently until they have been exposed repeatedly to an identical stimulus series under the same conditions of presentation (Tresselt and Volkmann, 1942). One of the well-known formulations in judgment today, designated in terms of the concept of *adaptation level* (Helson, 1947, 1948, 1959), is based precisely upon the determining role of stimulus values which the individual has encountered in the immediate and earlier past upon the level of his psychological scale of judgment.

Judgments of social stimuli, such as positions taken on a social issue, are also made in terms of a reference scale, a scale consisting of categorizations of the positions on the issue with end points defining extremist stands. Such scales are formed on the basis of encounters (firsthand and hearsay) with the stands represented on the issue.

All of the stimuli an individual has encountered may influence the placement of a particular item. However, certain items ordinarily exert a greater influence in determining its perceived position relative to the others. End points defining the extremes of a scale, or the value of a stimulus used repeatedly as a standard for judgment, exert greater influence than others. End points or other standards with greater effect in determining judgment of an item may be referred to as *anchorages* or simply as *anchors*. As we shall note later in this chapter, anchorages may be stimulus factors external to the individual, and they may also be internal, that is concepts or categories previously formed by the individual during the course of encounters with the stimuli in question.

The formation and functioning of reference scales seem basic for understanding judgments of verbal material as well as judgments of physical dimensions, such as weight, length, or area. In the present context, the discussion will concern the effect of stimulus conditions upon the formation of a reference scale and its principal properties.

Formation of Reference Scales Under Different Conditions

Specifications of stimulus arrangements and the properties of judgment scales formed relative to them have been most precise in laboratory studies of judgment. If we want to explore the topic, the laboratory is, therefore, the logical place to turn. Description of the stimulus arrangements in laboratory experiments could continue almost without end; however three modal conditions can be distinguished as more or less "pure" cases, in terms of procedures used in judgment experiments. Of course there are all manner of gradations and variations between them. These modal conditions can be distinguished as follows:

1. Formation of a scale on the basis of a well-graded stimulus series having an explicit standard within it.

2. Formation of a scale on the basis of a well-graded stimulus series without an explicit standard.

3. Formation of a scale without a graded stimulus series.

Each of these conditions and the principal properties of the resulting scales will be considered briefly in turn.

1. Stimulus series with explicit standard presented. This condition is exemplified by experiments using the *method of* "constant stimuli." A graded series of stimuli (say weights) is selected. These series stimuli ("comparison" or "variable" stimuli) are presented one at a time in random order on successive trials. With each series stimulus, a standard is presented, usually with a value near the middle stimulus of the series. For example, Bressler (1933) used eleven comparison weights ranging from 80 to 120 grams with a four-gram interval between successive stimuli and a standard weight of 100 grams. On every trial, the subject judges each stimulus in terms of the standard.

When the frequencies of judgments in each category are plotted against the stimulus series, there is considerable correspondence between stimulus series and judgment values, especially if certain precautions are used in selecting the standard stimulus (e.g. Woodrow, 1933, p. 415) and in the ordering of standard and series stimuli in presentation (e.g. Fernberger, 1920, 1931). However, as one might expect, judgment of stimuli with values near the standard is more accurate than at other regions of the scale. Since the standard is ordinarily an intermediate value relative to the series, this means that judgment is more accurate and less variable near the middle of the series. For example, Long (1937) reported greater stability, greater accuracy, and less "order effect" for judgments of stimuli around the average value in a study using sound intensities ranging from 20–40 decibels with a standard stimulus of 30 decibels (pp. 47f., 55).

As Woodworth and Schlosberg noted, the individual making judgments in this situation is ostensibly comparing a standard with each of a series of stimuli. "When he has become used to the range of Co[mparison] stimuli, however, each of them is likely to seem large, small, or medium in a quasi-absolute sense. . . . If the St[andard] were discon-

tinued, he could still go on using these categories confidently"
(1954, p. 217). Thus, a reference scale is more stable and
better fitted to stimulus values near the value of the standard
stimulus.

2. *Formation of judgment scale without explicit standard.*
It is of psychological, as well as historical, interest that the
formation of a psychological scale relative to a series of stimuli but without an explicitly introduced standard stimulus
had to be demonstrated (cf. Wever and Zener, 1928; Fernberger, 1931; Pfaffman, 1935). The procedure is termed the
method of single stimuli or, with considerable "terminolog-
ical unhappiness" (Volkmann, 1951), the "method of absolute stimuli." A series of stimuli (e.g. weights) is presented
to the subject for judgment one at a time with no standard
stimulus. He is instructed to give a judgment of, say, "one"
for the lightest, "six" for the heaviest, and numbers between
for others according to their perceived values. After a few
rounds of presentations, the subject places the stimuli in
their relative positions in the series, indicating the formation of a psychological scale with good fit, on the whole, to
the range and order of stimulus values of the series.

Without benefit of an explicit standard, how is it that the
subject can build a judgment scale corresponding to the range
and relative positions of the stimuli in the series? Let us try
to get an answer through a composite picture of what hap-
pens during an experiment with the method of single stimuli.
The first judgments are difficult for the subject—mere
guesses. After a few presentations of the series, the highest
and lowest stimulus values are identified and the end points
of the judgment scales are established. Then other stimuli
are placed according to their relative position between the
end points. Thus, Wever and Zener (1928) reported: "The
rapid growth of the absolute series is favored by the early
presentation of the extreme members of the body of stimuli"

(p. 473). And Needham (1935) concluded that the subject "first 'learns' to recognize the boundaries within which he is judging, and to assign to these limiting stimuli the relatively more correct judgments" (p. 282).

Thus, without an explicit standard, it is the end values of the series that ordinarily acquire an anchoring function. If so, we would expect that the psychological scale formed in this condition would be most stable, most accurate near the extreme stimulus values, as Needham found. Volkmann (1951) has also concluded that variability and errors of placement are greater for judgments of middle stimuli in the series, generalizing that the end stimuli control the oscillations of the psychological scale formed under these conditions.

Variability of judgments of intermediate stimuli is greater in the method of single stimuli than when a standard is introduced near the middle. In Wever and Zener's original experiment comparing the methods of single and constant stimuli, the striking difference was the much larger "intervals of uncertainty" for all subjects when an explicit standard was lacking. On the average, the interval of uncertainty was over half again greater without a standard (Wever and Zener, 1928, pp. 482, 484). Fernberger (1931) confirmed this finding (pp. 571, 578).

Thus, in comparison to a reference scale formed through encounters with a series and an explicit standard located near the middle of the series, the scale formed without an explicit standard is less stable, less accurate near the middle of the series. As a result, *judgments of intermediate stimuli are more subject to displacement* with a change in experimental procedures, such as rate of presentation (Needham, 1935). Individuals report uncertainty in judging the intermediate values, and their uncertainty is reflected in longer reaction times than for other judgment categories (Fernberger and Irwin, 1932). It is reasonable to conclude that different segments of the judgment scale acquire a different significance and vary in stability depending upon the conditions under which they were formed.

3. Reference scales formed in the absence of graded stimulus series. Having considered briefly the formation of judgment scales on the basis of encounters with series of well-graded stimuli with and without an explicit standard, let us consider the case in which a well-graded series is lacking as well. Such a situation is not infrequent in social life. Many social stimuli are complex and their major properties, from a psychological point of view, may not be clearly and obviously ordered along various dimensions through direct perceptual encounters with them, as, for example, a series of weights may be ordered by anyone with normal perceptual capacities who lifts them a number of times.

Judgments of the extent of perceived movements in the autokinetic situation are pertinent to the general problem. A small point of light visible in an otherwise dark place appears to move, even though it is completely stationary. Since autokinetic movement is not solely determined by the functioning of receptors (e.g. eye movements, retinal processes) but involves central processes (Crutchfield and Edwards, 1949), the extent of movement perceived is susceptible to internal influences from the individual himself and from social sources (e.g. instructions, judgments of others).

When an individual is presented the point of light for, say, one hundred trials in succession, his judgments of extent of movement become more or less stabilized within a range and around a characteristic modal value. From session to session, the individual maintains the range with diminishing variability (Sherif, 1935; Walter, 1955; Whittaker, 1958). While there is experimental evidence of a relationship between judged movement and individual personality (e.g. Voth,

1947), the point of emphasis here is the fact that individuals do stabilize a scale of judgment in such a situation over a period of time. Nor does this seem mysterious when the subjects' reports are considered. The following reports are representative of the ways subjects devise a basis for formation of their judgment scales: "First estimate as standard"; "Compared with previous distance"; "Approximated distance of spot from me, and used that"; "Compared successive judgments" (Sherif, 1935, p. 25).

When subjects establish their ranges of judgment individually and then speak their judgments aloud in each other's presence for a series of trials, their judgments tend to converge toward a common mode. Such convergence occurs even more rapidly if judgments are made in the presence of others from their first encounter with the situation. The common range attained in the social situation is maintained by the individuals when they judge *alone* on a subsequent day (Sherif, 1935) or even a considerable period of time later (Bovard, 1948; Rohrer et al., 1954).

Since the light, in this case, never moved in fact, it may appear that there are no limits to possible variations in judgment and the scales which various individuals might form under such a condition. Therefore, it should be stressed that the magnitude and range of judgments is not altogether independent of the stimulus conditions in which judgments are given. The objective conditions do set limits within which both individual and group variations in judgment take place. For example, under the usual procedure, the range for judgments of movement seldom exceeds eighteen inches for two-second exposures of the point of light five meters from the subject. Obtained ranges are increased by lengthening the exposure time and by putting greater distance between subject and light.

Compared to other conditions considered, however, the

formation of a judgment scale without a graded stimulus series is markedly influenced by internal anchors devised by the individual, if he judges alone, and by the judgments of other persons when estimates are made in a social situation.

Psychophysical and Psychosocial Scales of Judgment

The basis on which reference scales are formed is not merely an academic topic. The differential susceptibility to change of reference scales that the individual uses in categorizing and evaluating stimulus items is in part determined by the mode of their formation. Specifically, if we include in our consideration whether a given reference scale is formed in relation to objectively well-graded, well-structured stimulus objects with salient external anchors or in relation to items and topics that lack objective gradations, we gain effective leads in understanding why certain reference scales are more readily susceptible to change and others are more resistant to change. This consideration may be pertinent to the relatively greater susceptibility to change of norms in the technological sphere than in religious, political, and moral spheres, which social scientists discuss in terms of the concept of "cultural lag" (e.g. Ogburn, 1922, 1955; Herskovits, 1949).

As we have seen, when a series of stimuli are objectively well-graded with salient end points circumscribing the bounds of the series, the extent and category gradations of the ensuing reference scale correspond rather closely to the extent and gradations of the stimulus series. These psychophysical scales, so designated with reference to the mode of their formation, are readily susceptible to change and adjustments when the extent or gradations of the objective stimulus series change (Wever and Zener, 1928; Tresselt and Volkmann, 1942). Similarly the stimulus conditions involved in technological dimensions present objectively compelling gradations, and norms related to them are more readily susceptible to change, in line with the indications of judgment experiments.

Scales for categorizing stands on religious, moral, and social issues, which are more resistant to change, are psychosocial scales and are formed relative to stimuli which are not objectively well-graded. Therefore social factors, such as relationships with other people and the prevailing social outlook, are more compelling in determining the extent and categories of the reference scale. Not only are they formed relative to consequential aspects of living in groups—political, religious, economic, moral, social—but they become the regulating bases for the individual's evaluations of his relations with people, issues, and prevailing social practices.

Anchorages May Be Internal As Well As External

In this chapter we have referred to anchorages chiefly in discussing certain effects of an explicit standard stimulus and of end stimuli. However, it is well known in judgment research that a subject may use an internal standard (anchor) in judging a stimulus series presented in the laboratory. Such internal anchors may become operative in an experiment, for example, if the subject is instructed to think of his favorite color and use this as a standard in judging other colors. Laboratory experiments dealing with judgments as affected by internal anchors will be discussed in Chapter 4.

Problems of internal anchors are persistent in social judgment. In Part Two, we shall be dealing with the placement of verbal items and communications on social issues. When an individual has a strong stand on an issue, it may serve as a main anchorage for his judgments of items relevant to that issue. It is our aim to investigate displacements which may occur as a function of attitudinal anchors. Therefore we need to examine studies dealing with the *direction* of shifts produced by anchoring stimuli in the judgment of relatively simpler material.

CHAPTER 3

Interrelationships between Scales and Anchorages

LABORATORY STUDIES of relatively simpler judgments can clear the path for the study of social judgment by providing information concerning the effects of stimulus arrangements in situations where the principal determinants are easily observed and manipulated. In this chapter, our chief concern is the effect of the location relative to the reference scale of experimentally introduced anchorages upon the *direction* of shifts in judgment of relatively simple stimulus materials. The topic is pertinent to our general interest in the direction of attitudinal shifts with exposure to communication. In both instances, the location of an anchoring agent relative to a reference scale is involved.

DETERMINANTS IN PLACEMENT OF AN ITEM

As we have seen, judgment of a weight, of an inclination, or of the pleasantness of a color is determined by the interrelationships of a number of factors. Among factors determining placement of a stimulus item are (a) its objective value, (b) its relative place in a series, (c) the range of the series of which it is a part, and (d) the location of external and internal anchors relative to the series. In general, placement (appraisal) of an item in a stimulus series and the effects of an anchor introduced within or outside the limits of the series are determined by reciprocal relationships between the judgment scale and anchorages. Of course, this general statement will be qualified later for the case of ego-involving material, for the amount of familiarity with the material, and for certain characteristics of the stimulus material such as its relative structure or lack of structure.

In this chapter, our chief concern is the effect of the location of experimentally introduced anchorages relative to the reference scale upon the direction of shifts produced in judgment. We shall also consider the effect of the size of the stimulus range (wide or narrow) in relation to the position of the anchor, that is, values close to the stimulus series and remote from it. Finally, the chapter closes with a discussion of anchoring effects in the judgment of unstructured stimulus material.

Anchors Located Within and Outside the Series

Whether or not it is explicitly introduced by the experimenter, an anchor exerts considerable influence on the placement of items in a series. In the present discussion, the important problem is the effect of the location of the anchor within the stimulus series or outside it. The effect of location within the series was demonstrated strikingly in an experiment by Woodrow (1933), who used the usual fixed standard as well as varying standards in a weight-lifting study. He found reversals in "time-order" errors according to the position of the standard stimulus (anchor) within the series.

> With the varying standard procedure, the time-order errors, while on the whole negative, varied enormously with the 10 different weights given the standard. At its

> lightest weights, 110 grm. to 120 grm., all variables yielded *positive* time-order errors (corresponding to a difference in the percentages of "variable heavier" of 13); at weights 130 to 140 grm., the variables yielded an average time-order error of zero; while at weights from 150 to 200 grm. inclusive, all variables yielded negative time-order errors [p. 415].

The functional importance of the standard or anchor in a series is that other items are placed in relation to it. In the classical psychophysical experiment, the standard explicitly provided by the experimenter is usually located close to the center of the series. Accuracy is highest, variability is least, in the middle segment of the series, that is, where the standard or anchor is located (e.g. Fernberger, 1931; Long, 1937).

When no explicit standard is introduced within the series, accuracy and consistency of judgment are no longer characteristic of the middle segment, as noted in the last chapter. Thus under the single-stimuli procedure, the subject typically uses the end stimuli as anchors or standards for judgment. Consequently, the segment of the series for which judgments are more accurate and less variable shifts from the center segment (when standard is in the center) to the end segment (with no explicit standard).

An experiment reported by Volkmann illustrates the relative accuracy and variability of judgments for middle stimuli with the single-stimuli procedure (1951, pp. 281–4). In this experiment, subjects judged the area for each of a series of seven triangular forms, shape and brightness held constant. Subjects were instructed to give judgment *one* for the smallest area, *seven* for the largest area, and judgments of numbers in between for other areas, according to their size. Results reproduced in Figure 1 show that "errors pile up on the middle stimuli and middle categories." This finding was substantiated by other experiments of Reese, Reese, Volkmann, and Corbin (1953).

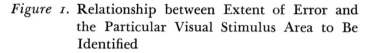

Figure 1. Relationship between Extent of Error and the Particular Visual Stimulus Area to Be Identified

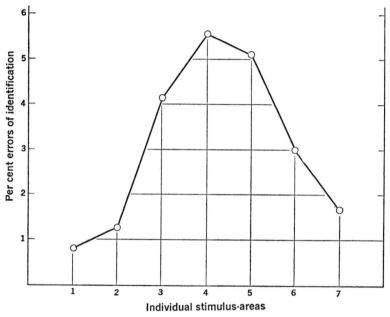

Note the piling up of errors in response to the middle stimuli. (From Volkmann 1951.)

On the basis of such findings, Volkmann draws a conclusion concerning the relative functional values of the end points and the middle segment for a judgment scale formed under single-stimuli procedures:

> The experiment has something else to tell us, however: it is primarily the *end-stimuli* that control the oscillations of the absolute scale. The center of the stimulus-range has no special functional significance

whatever. It is merely a convenient numerical value: the mean of the two end-stimuli. . . . We should not make the mistake of thinking that the operation of an absolute scale requires some implicit or averaged value equivalent in its effect to a standard stimulus. Indeed, . . . judgments are most variable (and consequently most likely to be in error) on the middle stimuli, exactly where an implicit standard might be located. Apparently it is not there [1951, p. 283].

More recently, experiments by Eriksen and Hake (1957) lend further weight to the above conclusion concerning the role of the end stimuli in placement of a series of magnitudes, even when subjects in different sessions were required to use different numerical categories for the end stimuli. In addition, subjects judged a "circular" series of hues which lacked objective end points. For this series, judgments using the first and last category numbers provided in instructions were more accurate than judgments using intermediate category numbers. Their significant generalization is that the end values of a stimulus series or, if they are lacking, the end categories used by the individual, determine the choice of a standard in making judgments (p. 137). In both cases selection of a basis for comparison by the individual is involved.

Noting Volkmann's emphasis upon the anchoring effect of end values in a series, Parducci, Calfee, Marshall, and Davidson (1960) performed a series of experiments in which range and frequency distribution of the stimuli presented for judgment were varied. Subjects judged the relative size of numerals presented simultaneously, using five categories. Shifts in judgment were associated with changes in the range (as indicated by the midpoint between the end stimuli) and changes in the frequency distribution (as indicated by the median of the stimuli presented). The authors suggest that the judgment scale formed for placement of such neutral items in an experimental situation is anchored by the end values and represents the joint effect of a tendency to divide the range into categories and to use the categories proportionate to the stimulus series presented.

The effect on placement of items of an anchor stimulus which recurs at every trial is convincingly shown by introducing an explicit anchor at some point in the stimulus series. The illustrative experiment is one of several on anchoring effects carried out at Mount Holyoke College (Volkmann, 1951, pp. 286–7). The stimulus series consisted of visual inclinations. The vertical was defined as zero-degree inclination. Without an explicit anchor, the mean error of placement at 30° from the vertical was about +6°. An anchor line at 30° was then introduced, and the subjects were informed that it was a 30° inclination. The introduction of the anchor reduced the error of placement in that segment of the series to nearly zero. "It is more important that errors of estimation decreased over a quite wide range of inclinations: from 5° to 40°. Above 40°, however, *the amount of this constant error was actually increased*" (p. 287, italics ours). Results from this experiment are shown in Figure 2.

In the report of another experiment from the Mount Holyoke College series, the direction of shifts in judgment with the introduction of an anchor is specified. The stimulus series consisted of "35 randomly arranged fields of dots ranging in number from 1 to 210." The task was estimation of the number of dots. The first part of the experiment was conducted without introducing an explicit anchor. Then, an anchor stimulus of 49 dots was introduced, and the subjects were informed of this fact. As in the above experiment, the percentage of error was reduced to almost zero in that segment. However, "there was a consistent tendency to overestimate stimuli below the anchor and to underestimate

stimuli above the anchor; the curve crosses the line of zero
per cent error at 49 dots" (Reese et al., 1953, p. 76). The net
result of both underestimation and overestimation in this
segment was shifts in placement toward the anchoring stimulus. On the other hand, beyond the segment in which the
anchor was introduced, errors in judgment and variability
increased. Of course, the judgment of large numbers of dots
with brief exposure times in this experiment was made by
estimating ("subitizing") rather than by actual counting.

Figure 2. Accuracy of Estimation of Visual Inclination

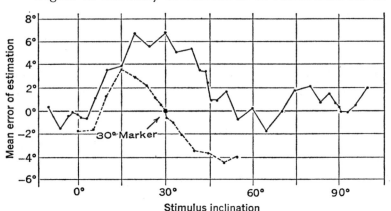

Note that the insertion of an anchoring stimulus at 30 degrees decreases
constant errors of estimation in the range from 5 to 40 degrees, but increases
errors outside that range. (From Volkmann 1951.)

Introduction of Anchoring Stimuli
Outside the Series

In an experiment by Rogers (1941), explicit anchoring
stimuli with values larger than any series stimuli were introduced for judgments of lifted weights and visual inclinations. As a result of anchors located at values increasingly
above the stimulus series, Rogers found shifts in judgment
values toward the lower categories, such that with the re-

motest anchors the upper categories dropped out of use. In the words of one subject, "all the stimuli look like 'ONE' " (i.e. like the lowest category). Rogers hypothesized that the subject was extending his "absolute scale" (psychological scale) upward toward the anchoring stimulus. Without making such assumptions, we can observe in his reported results that the *direction* of judgment shift following the introduction of remote anchors was *away* from the anchor value, and that larger categories dropped out of use. Subsequently Postman and Miller (1945) and Heintz (1950) reported judgment shifts *away* from the values of remote anchors and demonstrated that the effect was not dependent upon explicit introduction of the anchor stimulus as representative of a given category or upon pairing the anchor with a series stimulus on each presentation (although the frequency with which the anchor is presented does influence the magnitude of its effect). McGarvey (1943) reported similar results for the placement of verbal statements.

In terms of our present interest, it is noteworthy that displacement *away* from the value of another stimulus is not exclusively the result of introducing anchor stimuli located outside a stimulus series. A rather impressive list of experiments report such displacements when stimuli of widely differing values are presented successively or simultaneously. Long (1937) found such displacements in studying the effects of preceding auditory intensities upon the judgment of succeeding intensities, and noted their presence in experiments employing a variety of stimuli, including tones, weights, colors, and odors. The phenomenon is the well-known *contrast effect,* that is, a shift in judgment *away* from the value of another stimulus to which it is related in kind (dimension) and temporal occurrence.

The contrast phenomenon is of interest to us because, as shall be seen in detail later, similar displacements occur in

the appraisal of socially relevant material. In addition, shift
in judgment toward another stimulus value sometimes occurs
when material on a social issue is evaluated; it may be said
that this is one of the aims of persuasive communications, for
example. Therefore, it seems worthwhile to attempt to
analyze the direction of shifts in judgment in functional
terms applicable to a variety of stimulus material. In doing
so, we will try to avoid assumptions not indicated by the
data. For example, the data do not give evidence that the
individual extends his scale and its categories to cover a
continuum stretching from the series to a remote anchor;
he reports that as far as he is concerned, the stimuli which
previously were placed in the end categories nearest the
anchor are simply missing (e.g. Heintz, 1950; Rogers, 1941).

Through functional analysis of relationships between
stimulus series and anchors located within and outside the
series, it may be possible to derive leads useful for understanding shifts in social judgments as well. Since anchorages
for social judgments are frequently internal and value-laden,
an analysis based on a region of neutrality or indifference
does not seem entirely appropriate for significant problems
in the social field. Social standards or norms, for example,
may set a level for judgments of social behavior, but they
hardly represent regions of neutrality or indifference. On
the contrary, they define a range of the *expected,* the *desired,*
and even the *ideal* (Sherif, 1948; Sherif and Sherif, 1956).

Direction of shifts. For purposes of functional analysis,
shifts in placement produced by an anchor located within or
outside a series of stimuli can be labeled in terms of the *direction* of the shifts. As we have seen, judgment shifts are
reported both *toward* and *away* from an anchor value. We
shall designate the shift in placement of a stimulus toward
an anchor value as *assimilation,* and shifts in placement of a
stimulus away from an anchor value as a *contrast effect.* In

short, these labels describe direction of shift for the purpose of making a functional analysis of the factors and relationships producing systematic shifts in judgment.

Our usage is stressed because at times "assimilation" is used differently in physiological explanation of the time-order error, and because at times the contrast phenomena found upon introduction of remote anchoring stimuli are treated in terms of hypothetical shifts ("extensions") of the psychological scale toward the anchor. In view of two different usages of the term "assimilation" in judgment literature, some authors have been cautious in using it to refer to obtained displacements of series stimuli toward the anchor. They refer to such shifts simply as the "reverse" of contrast (Long, 1937, pp. 40, 54; Guilford, 1954, p. 280).

An Experimental Research Program

In order to seek general principles from judgment studies and to test their applicability to attitude and attitude change problems using controversial social issues, a research attack on judgment was undertaken by the Yale Communication and Attitude Change Program. As indicated earlier, our aim was a functional analysis applicable both to the study of relatively simple judgments and to the study of appraisals of verbal communication. One of the schemes appearing applicable to both was analysis in terms of reciprocal effects of scales and anchorages. This analysis should include the interrelationships among values and properties of stimulus items, their range, the relative position of particular items, and anchors (both external and internal) (cf. Sherif, 1947).

In this chapter we shall discuss certain hypotheses concerning reciprocal effects of scales and anchorages on the direction of shifts in judgment for relatively simple and motivationally neutral stimulus material. The first experiment deals with the effects of anchors whose location (close and remote) relative to a stimulus series is systematically varied. The second concerns judgments of stimuli in a "wide" series and in a "narrow" stimulus series and the effects of anchors at given locations outside each series. The third experiment varies the location of anchors relative to psychological scales formed by subjects in judging an unstructured stimulus situation.

A Scheme for Studying Judgment Scales and Anchorages

Figure 3 presents schematically the effect of an anchor on placement of stimuli in a series, when the anchor is placed at a given location within or outside the stimulus series. In this highly simplified scheme, placement is represented by median judgment values. Two different stimulus series (A and B) are represented.

In interpreting this scheme, we start with a stimulus series with a specific range, as indicated in A and B by the segment demarcated by two heavy lines and designated RSS. The location of an anchor stimulus of the same dimension is shown by an arrow ↓. We assume here that only one anchor is used during one experimental session. Median judgment values for each of the series (A and B) are represented along the ordinate plotted against the differing anchor values introduced in different sessions.

The range of anchor values within which assimilation may occur is represented by the positively inclined portion of the curve and is bounded by broken vertical lines. This portion of the curve extends slightly beyond the stimulus values of the lower and upper ends of the stimulus series (RSS). The assimilation range beyond the two ends of the stimulus series is small in comparison with the contrast range. Since the assimilation effect implies perceived resemblance or similarity, it occurs within a limited range in judgment of stimulus series with discriminable differences particularly in motivationally neutral dimensions. It is assumed that the assimilation range varies with the nature of stimulus items being

Figure 3. Hypothetical Curves Showing Ranges of Assimilation and of Contrast with Narrow (Series A) and with Wide (Series B) Ranges of Stimulus Series

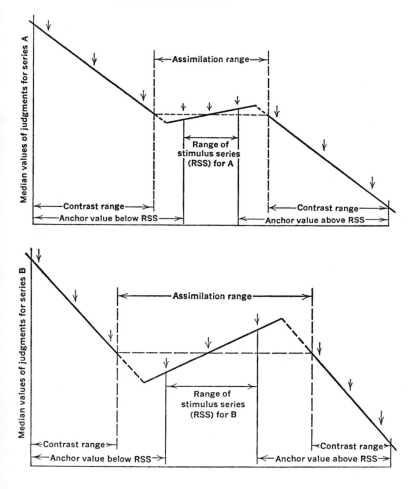

judged. The assimilation range is narrow for well-defined physical continuums in which discriminability is sharp (Weber ratio is small). The range of assimilation is much larger when judgments concern unstructured stimulus material (pp. 63–67).

For judgments of verbal material toward which the individual has an established attitude, the assimilation range may be larger than here represented, depending both on the individual's attitude (which functions as an internal anchorage) and the relative ambiguity of the items. When neutral items or items representing intermediary positions between extremes are included, assimilation is mediated through shifts in placement of these items. (The latter possibilities, not represented in these figures, are discussed in later chapters. Here we may mention that the effects vary with the stimulus material and with the subject's internal anchorage, or attitude, e.g. the range of positions on a social issue which he includes in his "latitude of acceptance" and the degree of his ego-involvement.)

The contrast range is not as restricted as the assimilation range. A contrast effect is produced by *differences* between two or more stimuli being compared on a given dimension. However, the contrast range may not extend along a given dimension indefinitely. When differences between two objects are extreme, they may not be perceived as two objects differing along a given dimension, but rather as belonging to two entirely different universes.

Although there have not been systematic investigations of the limitations of the contrast range, there is some suggestive experimental evidence. Brown (1953), for example, reported that stimuli differing in other dimensions from items being judged produced no anchoring effects unless subjects were instructed to judge them on the same dimension. Parducci (1954) found that when subjects made judgments of size and were also required to judge an anchor stimulus differing in both size and color, the anchoring effect was smaller than when anchor stimuli differed from the series in size only. In other words, for anchoring effects to occur, the subject has to perceive anchors as related to series stimuli. Perhaps the weakening of the series-anchor relationship is responsible for Postman and Miller's finding in temporal judgment that the "introduction of more and more remote anchors yields only diminishing returns" (1945, p. 49). Such "diminishing returns" were not found by Heintz (1950), but it is possible that his most remote anchor did not differ from the largest series stimulus sufficiently to make a test. The extent of the contrast range for judgments on a given dimension would seem to have some bearing on social judgments by individuals with different reference scales, say, for standard of living.

Anchors have been introduced within the stimulus series in several experiments as well as beyond the ends of the series. Concerning their effect, Guilford concludes: "Anchors *within* the stimulus range, when not balanced around a central stimulus value, have effects like those outside the range" (1954, p. 313). The use of anchors within the stimulus series is functionally equivalent to the use of a *standard* stimulus in classical psychophysical methods (cf. Helson, 1959, p. 595). The standard is ordinarily located near the middle stimulus value, with variations designed to correct constant errors. The effects of the standard used in psychophysical methods may be considered as special cases of anchoring effects. Therefore, one could refer to the anchors represented within the stimulus series in Figure 3 as "standards."

Effects of Anchors at Varying Locations

The three-part experiment to be summarized here studied the relation between the direction of shifts in judgment and the position of anchor stimuli within or outside a stimulus series (Sherif, Taub, Hovland, 1958). In line with the scheme presented above, the hypotheses were:

1. In judgments of graded stimuli ranging from low to high in some dimension, the introduction of anchors at the end points of the series, or immediately above or below the series, will cause displacement of the distribution of judgments *in the direction of the anchor* ("assimilation effect").

2. As the anchors are placed at increasing distances from the upper or lower ends of the series, the distribution of judgments will be displaced in the direction *away from the anchor* and the judgment scale will be constricted to fewer categories ("contrast effect").

The procedure and instructions in the first part of the study followed rather closely those used by Rogers (1941) in his study of anchoring effects for judgments of lifted weights. In the second part of the study, two additional series of weights were used, with anchor weights located at and below the lighter end of the series. A session without introduced anchors came first (original series). Only subjects who correctly discriminated the original stimulus series in at least 50 per cent of the trials were used in subsequent sessions. In the nine anchor sessions which followed, only one anchor was used during a single session. The order of the anchor sessions was randomized.

The principal results are shown in Figure 4. The distributions of judgments for the no-anchor session and for various anchor sessions are indicated. It will be observed that judgments in the no-anchor session are rather evenly distributed along the six categories with a slight piling up in categories *four* and *five*. When an anchor whose value in grams corresponds to the value of the top stimulus in the series is introduced, the concentration of judgments in the upper

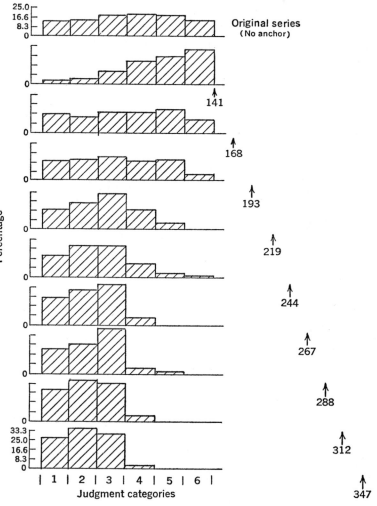

Figure 4. Distribution of Judgments for Series of Weights without Anchor (Top) and with Anchors at Increasing Distances above Original Series (Bottom)

Position of anchor indicated by arrows. (From Sherif, Taub, and Hovland 1958.)

categories is considerably increased, that is, the shift is *toward the anchor value.* Starting with the anchor of 193
grams, more distant anchors tend increasingly to produce the
opposite effect, causing a displacement of judgments to the
lower end of the scale and *away from the anchor.* These effects hold for each of the individual subjects with only
minor variations.

The effects of anchors increasingly distant from the top
of the original stimulus series can be represented more
clearly by plotting the median judgment given to the
stimulus series without anchor and with the different anchors
at varying distances from the original stimulus series. This
method of presenting the results is given in Figure 5.

The median judgment during the original series without
anchor is used as the baseline from which to evaluate changes.
It will be observed that compared with this value there is an
upward displacement of the median judgment value for the
same stimulus series when the anchor is close to the series
and a displacement away from the anchor value when it is
more remote. The former is the anticipated "assimilation
effect" and the latter the "contrast effect."

The preceding results indicate the assimilation and contrast effects predicted for anchors at varying locations above
the stimulus series. It seemed desirable to replicate the experiment in order to determine whether the same effects
would also be obtained when anchors are introduced at the
lower end of the original series. This was done in a supple-
mentary experiment that was carried out in two separate
units using different series of weights, designated as Series
I and II.

The distributions of judgments obtained for Series I, with
anchors at varying distances from the series, are shown in
Figure 6. It will be noted that both the 75-gram anchor and
the 71-gram anchor, which were slightly below the end

stimulus, produced shifts in the distribution toward the anchor ("assimilation"). Anchors further removed from the end (43 and 35 grams) produced a shift in the opposite direction ("contrast"), although not as pronounced as the similar trend in the first part of the experiment.

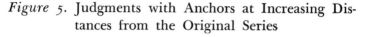

Figure 5. Judgments with Anchors at Increasing Distances from the Original Series

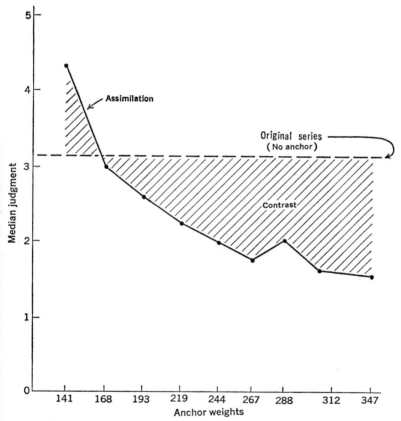

Shaded area indicates deviation from values for original series without anchor. (From Sherif, Taub, and Hovland 1958.)

Figure 6B shows the distributions of judgments obtained for Series II for no-anchor and anchor sessions. It appears quite clear that an assimilation effect occurs in the lower range with the first anchor and the anchor just below the series. Anchors further below resulted in contrast effects much like those obtained in the first part.

Figure 6. Distribution of Judgments for Two Different ent Stimulus Series without Anchor and with Anchors at Varying Distances below Each Series

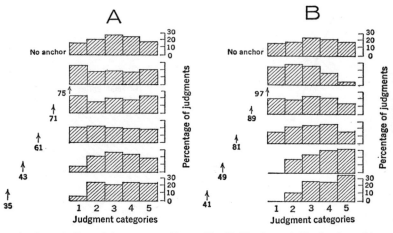

Anchors indicated by arrows. (From Sherif, Taub, and Hovland 1958.)

It is a little difficult to compare our findings with those of Rogers. He did not anticipate an assimilation effect and did not include results obtained under the no-anchor condition in his presentation. From inspection of his table giving mean scale values for two subjects (Rogers, 1941, p. 32), it appears that with the anchor placed at the top of the series there was a trend toward larger than usual scale values for most of the stimuli in the series.

Postman and Miller (1945), however, reported a reversal

in trend which is worth noting, although not statistically significant. They obtained temporal judgments for a series of five durations (250, 375, 750, and 1,000 ms.) under no-anchor and anchor conditions. Anchor durations were 1,000, 1,150, 1,400, and 1,500 ms. The experimenters did not instruct their subjects that the anchor stimulus represented the top judgment category. (This procedure is more in harmony with a major assumption of the single-stimuli procedure: that stimuli are judged in relation to one another even in the absence of an *explicit* anchor.) With remote anchors, the usual contrast effects were obtained, i.e. shifts away from anchor. But in the case of the first anchor, there was a slight shift toward the anchor, which constituted a reversal of the trend obtained for the other anchors. It would be interesting to plot anchoring effects using smaller steps between anchor values in the region bordering the end values of the stimulus series.

In a study systematically changing the series relative to a heavy or light anchor, Helson and Nash (1960) found increasing shifts in judgment away from a remote anchor as the series values diverged increasingly. The finding is particularly noteworthy since anchor stimuli were *not* designated as standards, and subjects were permitted to add categories at either end of the scale if they wished. The contrast effect occurred whether the series judged first was composed of stimuli nearest the anchor value or most divergent from it; however, there seem to have been small interaction effects between order of change in the series and anchor effect. The judgment of stimuli nearest the anchor was affected more than the judgment of those remote from it. Since it was not the purpose of the experiment to analyze relative frequencies of judgment values, it is not feasible to detect possible assimilation effects which might be expected with the least discrepancy between anchor and series values.

Range of the Series and Anchor Values

Both on theoretical grounds and from empirical observations, it might be expected that the size of the stimulus range would affect the way the individual perceives a particular anchor stimulus. More generally, the series stimulus range and anchor value should reciprocally affect the placement of particular items, jointly influencing the size and direction of displacements toward or away from anchor values (Sherif, 1947).

In other words, it might be predicted that anchoring effects are jointly determined by their relative distance from the stimulus series and by the range of the stimulus series as well. If so, anchor stimuli with the same values would have differing effects on judgments of stimulus series with narrow and wide ranges. An experiment by Harvey and Campbell (1960) carried out as a unit in the Yale Attitude and Communications Research Program is suggestive in this regard.

Anchoring Effects for Two Series with Different Ranges

In Harvey and Campbell's experiment, two stimulus series were presented in which the middle weights were identical but the values of end stimuli and consequently the differences between adjacent series stimuli were different. The end stimuli of the narrow series (361.9–507.8 grams) were intermediary stimuli in the wide series (305.5–601.5 grams). The anchor values, one lighter and one heavier, introduced in a second session were both quite discrepant from the end values of the two series. The study has a bearing on the reciprocal effects upon shifts in judgment of series range and location of anchors. The design does not permit a definite test of the role of series range relative to anchor position since the anchors had the same absolute values and there-fore varied in position relative to the two series.

In addition to series range and anchor position, the ex-periment varied amount of practice with the series in the first session (10 or 25 trials). Thus series range, amount of practice, and anchor values were varied in a 2x2x2 factorial design. In addition, each of the eight variable conditions was replicated with instructions to make judgments in ounces and to make judgments in five categories. Subjects were not instructed about the anchor but were expected to judge it along with the series stimuli.

The main results can be summarized as follows. The judg-ments of the middle weight common to both series did not differ significantly in the context of the different series. How-ever, judgments of the other two weights common to the two series did differ before anchors were introduced. As end stimuli in the narrow range, these weights were judged lighter and heavier, respectively, than they were when inter-mediary stimuli in a wider range. The differences were signif-icant only when the subjects used numbers as category labels.

The introduction of anchoring stimuli produced the ex-pected contrast effects. Judgments of all weights common to the series shifted away from the anchors, the extent of shift being greater for the narrow series, the more remote anchor, and for stimuli at the end of the scale closest to the anchor position.

The extent of shift owing to the anchor was less when judgments were given in ounces, a finding the authors at-tribute to the unbounded availability of new categories. However, the effect of the anchor upon accuracy was not significantly different whether ounces or category numbers were used. Nor did amount of practice prior to introduction of the anchor affect discrimination, although series width and heaviness of anchor did. Accuracy was most affected for the narrow series and heavier anchor. It is interesting that with the reduced accuracy, variability of judgment also decreased with the introduction of the anchor.

Finally the authors report that amount of practice with the series significantly affected placement of the anchor stimulus. Of course, placement of the anchor also differed according to its objective size, and there were significant interaction effects between size of the series range and anchor magnitude.

The results of the experiment suggest the value of further investigations of reciprocal relationships between stimulus range and relative discrepancy of the anchor. They also indicate that shifts in judgment associated with discrepant anchor values are not artifacts of experimental instructions.

Anchoring Effects and Category Availability

Several experiments indicate that anchoring effects are not merely a function of the particular categories available to the subject rendering a judgment. For example, Long (1937) reported assimilation and contrast effects when subjects judged in physical units, as did Harvey and Campbell in the study just summarized. Helson and Nash (1960) instructed subjects not to use the discrepant "background" weight paired with each series stimulus as a standard and further instructed them to add categories if they wished.

On the other hand, it is reasonable to suppose that the availability of concepts is an important variable in judgment, and the problem is pertinent to social judgment. Linguistic structure, vocabulary, cultural norms, and individual experiences may limit or extend the categories available for judging a social dimension.

Recently, B. J. White (1960) systematically varied the

number and location of categories available for judgments of a series of weights by the method of single stimuli and following the introduction of a discrepant (much lighter) anchor. In one condition, White introduced the anchor but made no more categories available, so that there was one less category than weights to be judged. In a second, a single additional category was made available when the anchor was introduced. In a third condition, three additional categories were provided, but at the light end of the scale near the anchor. In all three of these conditions, judgments shifted away from the light anchor and the judgment scale was constricted, i.e. the lighter categories dropped out of use.

Under a fourth condition White instructed subjects that they might use three additional categories at the end of the judgment scale farthest removed from the anchor. As a final condition, three additional categories were provided at *each* end of the scale. In both conditions, subjects shifted their entire judgment scale upward to the "heavier" categories, away from the light anchor. Thus the contrast effect occurred, but not through piling up judgments into fewer categories. Even judgments of the heavy end stimulus shifted significantly.

To summarize, White found significant displacement of judgments away from the remote anchor in every condition, the extent of the contrast effect being greatest for those conditions in which additional categories were provided at the end of the scale most remote from the anchor. Constriction of the judgment scale to fewer categories following introduction of an anchor was found only in those conditions restricting categories for judgment.

The psychological significance of categories available for judgment is suggested in Eriksen and Hake's findings (1957) reported earlier in this chapter. In their experiment, anchoring effects owing to compelling stimulus properties (e.g.

clearly being the "smallest" or "largest" of a series) were reproduced by category designation relative to a series of colors
with no obvious limits. The authors propose that in both
instances the subject selects given items as standards for judgment, the selection being determined by category names more
decisively when compelling stimulus properties cannot guide
the choice. Doubtless the latter is the case in many social
judgments, in which groups may differ in categories assigned
a particular item and even in the ordering of items in comparative categories.

Anchoring Effects in Judgment of Unstructured Situations

Now we consider anchoring effects on a scale for judgment
formed in relation to a stimulus situation lacking a well-
graded series (cf. Chapter 2, p. 34). The formation of psychosocial scales is typically of this kind. As previously noted,
evidence for the existence of a judgment scale pertaining to
such stimulation is the finding that the individual does, in
time, distribute his judgments within a definite range and
around a modal point which is maintained with reduced
variability on subsequent occasions. Experimental variation
of the anchor location is made relative to the particular individual's own judgment scale which he formed on initial
contact with the situation.

Location of anchor position can be specified by introducing
a "planted" subject who speaks aloud a series of judgments
prescribed by the experimenter. Shifts in judgment toward
or away from the anchor value are often labeled "convergence" and "divergence" or "deviation." In terms of direction of shift, "convergence" and "assimilation" are of course
identical, as are "divergence" and "contrast."

The reciprocal relations between scales and anchors in
such experimental settings may be representative of situations

in which the stimulus lacks structure and in which the judgment dimension and ordering of items along it are socially defined. In social life, individuals utilize available evidence in making judgments, including appraisals by other individuals and groups. To the extent that determinate physical evidence is lacking, the likelihood of reliance on judgments of other persons increases (e.g. Coffin, 1941; Luchins, 1944; Thrasher, 1954). Thus when naive individuals initially judge an unstructured situation in each other's presence, judgments rapidly converge toward a common range, which is maintained at a later time when the individuals are alone (Sherif, 1935).

It might appear that assimilation to an anchor (spoken judgments of another person) in judgment of a dimension such as apparent movement would be likely, regardless of the size of the differences between the individual's own judgment scale and the anchor location. Sperling (in Asch, 1952), however, found negligible shift toward a plant's judgments when their values were much greater than the subject's. Indirectly, objective conditions affect the assimilation range for judgments of autokinetic movement by limiting the range of the judgment scale. Such objective conditions include the distance between the light and the subject, the exposure time, the subject's impression of the size of the room from its location in the building, the amount of echo, etc.

Therefore, it seemed reasonable to predict that anchoring effects in judgments of the autokinetic situation would vary in terms of the reciprocal relations between scales and anchors in much the same fashion as judgments of well-graded series, but with markedly different assimilation and contrast ranges. In other words, the direction and extent of judgment shift should vary with the distance between the individual's scale and the location of the anchor, the extent of shift toward the anchor bearing an inverse relationship to this distance.

This proposition was recently investigated in an experiment which is summarized below.

Varying Anchor Location for Judgments of Autokinetic Movement

The general hypothesis of the experiment by J. O. Whittaker (1958) was that the extent of judgment shift in the direction of the spoken judgments of a planted subject would vary inversely with the discrepancy between the individual's judgment scale and the plant's judgments.

The experiment was carried out in a dark room with a pin point of light located 18 feet from the subject and a two-second exposure after movement was first reported. In the first session of the experiment, each naive subject individually made 40 judgments of apparent movement. In the second session 48 hours later, the following experimental conditions were introduced:

Condition A (*Control*): Subjects again made judgments alone as in session 1.

Condition B (*Anchor 1*): Subjects served with plant who made judgments around a median one inch higher than subject's largest judgment in session 1.

Condition C (*Anchor 2X*): Subjects served with plant who made judgments ranging upward from a value twice the subject's largest judgment in session 1.

Condition D (*Anchor 8X*): Subjects served with plant who made judgments ranging upward from a value eight times the subject's largest judgment in session 1.

Condition E (*Anchor 12X*): Subjects served with plant who made judgments ranging upward from a value twelve times the subject's largest judgment in session 1.

Ten subjects served in each condition, the plant being the same individual in each. Regardless of the plant's median in a given condition, he distributed his judgments within a range equal in size to that of the particular subject in session 1.

Subjects serving under Condition A (Control) tended to distribute their judgments around the same medians in session 1 and session 2 with reduced variability. The average (mean) shift in medians was —.28. A comparison of mean shift with anchors 1, 2X, 8X, and 12X is given in Figure 7, adapted from Whittaker. The mean shift in judgment toward anchor decreased from 4.07 with anchor 1, to 3.09 for anchor 2X, to only .42 for anchor 8X, and .13 for anchor 12X.

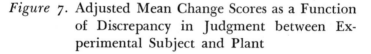

Figure 7. Adjusted Mean Change Scores as a Function of Discrepancy in Judgment between Experimental Subject and Plant

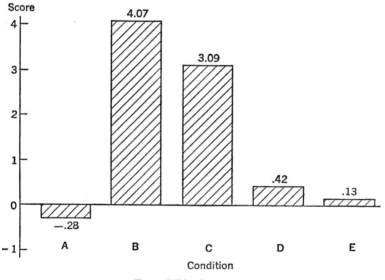

(From Whittaker 1958.)

Mean shifts toward anchor 1 and toward anchor 2X both differed significantly from shifts toward anchors 8X and 12X. However, differences in absolute shifts with anchor 1 and anchor 2X were not significant nor were those between anchors 8X and 12X. In terms of shift proportional to the distance between the subject's median and the plant's median, however, the difference in shifts with anchor 1 and anchor 2X was significant.

Whittaker's analysis of the variability of judgments was related to previous reports by Kelman (1950) and Walter (1955) that the acceptance of a standard for judgment reduces variability. Whittaker reported that variability increased significantly when anchors 1 and 2X were introduced. He considered this increased variability indicative of uncertainty created by anchors at considerable distances from the subject's judgment scale, a conclusion supported by a significant difference in confidence judgments for sessions 1 and 2. On the other hand, with the introduction of anchors 8X and 12X, variability of judgments was reduced, and confidence in judgments was higher. The introduction of remote anchors produced a contrast effect in the judgments of several subjects with shifts *away* from anchors 8X and 12X. No such shifts away from the anchor occurred with anchors 1 or 2X.

On the basis of this experiment, it may be concluded that the range of assimilation is far greater in judgments of unstructured stimulus materials, but that the extent of assimilation varies with the distance between the judgment scale and the anchor position. The results support the hypothesis that this variation follows an inverse relationship: with increased discrepancy between judgment scale and anchor position, the extent of shift toward the anchor decreases, dwindling almost to the zero point with the most remote anchor.

The anchor source in this experiment was a stranger. By

varying prestige and perceived "success" of the source, the assimilation range would probably extend beyond that obtained in Whittaker's experiment. On the other hand, shifts *away* from anchor source in judgments of unstructured stimulus situations have been obtained by procedures reducing the credibility of the source or increasing the subject's confidence in his own judgments. We will summarize some of the relevant findings in the following chapter. Meanwhile, it may be observed that the suggestive indication of "contrast" reported by Whittaker for some subjects exposed to the most remote anchors might become a dominant direction of shift if the subject perceives the plant's spoken judgments as wrong, or as extremely irritating.

We will proceed now to a discussion of factors not discussed thus far, such as practice, attitude, and ego-involvement. Then we can apply our analysis of the functional relationships between scales and anchors to the more complicated situations involving communication on a social issue.

CHAPTER 4

Internalized Reference Scales and Anchors

THE MAJOR FINDINGS from judgment studies summarized in Chapter 2 pertained to the formation of judgment scales under different arrangements of external stimuli. After repeated encounters with a range of stimuli, a reference scale is established which henceforth provides an internal basis for comparison. How standards which were originally external become internalized and their effects on reaction to relevant stimulus material will be discussed in the present chapter. Also interaction of scales and anchors discussed in the last chapter will be illustrated through experiments utilizing ego-involving dimensions.

INTERNAL ANCHORS IN JUDGMENT EXPERIMENTS

When an individual comes to the laboratory to make judgments of pitch, weight, inclination, numerousness, or odor, it can usually be assumed that he has had some prior experience with the stimulus dimension. Thus individual differences in early judgments attributable to previous encounters are often found and may persist throughout an experiment. In the latter case, the individual's reference scale for the dimension is presumably well established on the basis of prior experience. Ordinarily, however, the judgments of different individuals become more uniform as they are exposed repeatedly to the same graded series (Tresselt and Volkmann, 1942). From this finding, it is inferred that the individuals have learned the series; they have internalized a reference scale composed of categories provided by the experimenter on the basis of repeated encounters with the series.

The postulation of an internalized reference scale is supported by the results of introducing a new or expanded series of stimuli. The sudden introduction of new stimuli differing in value (greater or less) from an established series results in increased error in predictable directions which persists for several rounds of presentation of the series. This was noted by Wever and Zener (1928) in their early study of single-stimuli procedures and has been confirmed by Tresselt (1947), Nash (1952), and Parducci (1954), among others.

As we have seen in Chapter 3, the effects of anchoring stimuli introduced after the establishment of a judgment scale for a specified range of stimuli depends jointly upon the scale and the location of the anchors. These anchoring effects are not confined to reactions to external anchor stimuli, however. Some years ago, Volkmann (1936) demonstrated judgment shifts in response to an *internal* anchor. After judging a series of visual inclinations, his subjects were instructed to think of an inclination greater than any presented to them thus far and to let that inclination define what they called category "one." Their subsequent judgments were influenced as though a remote anchor stimulus had actually been presented. Thus internal factors, in this case a conceptual category produced by instructions, can function as anchors in judgment.

Subsequently, Hunt and Volkmann (1937) reported similar phenomena in affective judgments. A series of colored papers was presented to be placed in categories from "one" to

"seven," the higher numbers representing the pleasant segment of the scale. The instruction was to "think of the most
pleasant color you can" and "let its pleasantness define the
step 'seven' on your scale." As a result, placement of the
series colors shifted *away* from the "most pleasant" anchor,
that is, toward the unpleasant end of the scale.

Hunt (1941) then studied shifts in judgment as a consequence of internal anchors located outside the experimental
series using more complex material. The experiments included affective judgments of colors, aesthetic judgments of
ivory carvings and modern paintings, intelligence ratings of
children's faces, and normative judgments of crimes in terms
of the degree of violation involved. In some instances the
instructions introduced verbal anchors below the lowest category (most unpleasant or objectionable) and, in others, anchors above the highest category (most favored or acceptable).
The over-all findings confirm the earlier results. Specifically,
when the subject uses an internal anchor above the series,
judgments shift downward away from the anchor; the shift
is upward when the anchor lies below the lower end of the
series.

A *contrast effect* occurs when the discrepancy between the
internal anchor and series stimuli is large. However, when
an item within the series resembles the internal anchor in
some respect, shifts of judgment *toward* the anchor result
(cf. Peak, 1958, p. 335). Shifts toward the anchor, that is, an
assimilation effect, are illustrated by Hunt: "Keeping in mind
the least intelligent child he had ever seen would raise O's
judgments of most of the pictures, until he suddenly noticed
that one of the children in some way resembled the unintel-
ligent child he had in mind. Then this child would be
judged as much less intelligent than previously" (1941,
p. 401). In other words, the shift would be in the direction
of the internal anchor.

An observation by Hunt in his experiments on affective judgments of complex stimuli contains a hint of one additional phenomenon to be handled: "Occasionally, the addition of an anchor value at one extreme of the scale results in O's spontaneously adding one of his own at the opposite extreme. Such an addition results in a compression from both ends of the scale, with very little, if any, shift in central tendency" (p. 403).

When the objects of judgment are relevant to the individual's attitudes, his spontaneous and uninstructed use of internal anchors becomes a persistent and central problem. The phenomenon may occur even when subjects are instructed not to use internal anchors. Fifty years ago, Wells (1907) gave an example of displacements produced by the spontaneous functioning of internal standards. He observed that in estimations of scientific merit, psychologists tended to "give disproportionately high positions to men engaged in the same special work with them and to their own immediate colleagues" (p. 26). In further study of literary merit, he noted that the standards producing displacements were not those in the instructions and not necessarily those which the subjects listed when asked to specify their standards. He concluded that the use of unspecified internal standards (anchors) was a major source of these displacements. In contrast with errors in varying directions due to task difficulty, the errors resulting from internal standards occurred in a constant direction for a given individual.

A recent study by Perloe (1960) found contrast effects in judgments of occupational prestige even though the subjects had not been instructed to refer their judgments to their own status level. In comparison with the results of a nationwide survey of occupational prestige, high status individuals (Yale students) displaced the prestige of occupations at the middle and lower ranks away from their own high status.

Perloe attributes this contrast effect to "high status (Yale) Ss using their own actual or expected positions on the occupational prestige dimension as internal anchors" (p. 6).

The continuity of findings on anchor effects from judgments of neutral items to affective items may serve as a bridge to the study of social judgment. On this basis, new factors can be handled without invoking wholly new principles. For example, Berkowitz (1960) recently made a serious attempt to "show that judgmental principles uncovered in the psychophysics laboratory and recently extended to social evaluation situations can also be applied to personality functioning. These principles deal with judgmental contrast and assimilation, and it is proposed, for example, that psychoanalytic projection is readily understood as a special instance of these phenomena" (p. 141). Similarly, Campbell, Hunt, and Lewis (1957) have studied the conditions affecting assimilation and contrast effects in clinical judgments of degree of disturbance manifested in behavior samples by schizophrenic subjects.

In this book, we have proceeded with caution, concentrating first on categorizations and anchor effects in judgment of simpler verbal materials before undertaking the more complex problems of categorizations on complex social issues (Chapters 5–7). This is necessary if our task is to define essential similarities in judgment of relatively neutral and attitudinal items in terms of relationships between reference scales and anchors.

The Acquisition of Scales and Anchors Through Learning

If the reference scale for judgment is closely related to the range of stimulation to which the individual is exposed, it should be possible to produce differential internalization experimentally and to demonstrate differences in judgment as a consequence. In order to study this problem, Tresselt (1947) presented a series of twelve weights to different groups of subjects who had previously had varying amounts of practice with the four heaviest weights or the four lightest weights in the series. Analysis of the "medium" judgments for the entire series led Tresselt to conclude: "There is a definite effect of different amounts of practice upon the first judgment of stimuli in the expanded stimulus-range. The greater the amount of practice, the more slowly does the scale of judgment shift to its new position" (p. 260). As the subjects were exposed to the total stimulus range, their judgment scales came to correspond with the expanded series. One subject, however, did not alter his scale. He lifted heavy weights for recreation and called all weights light throughout the experiment.

Therefore, Tresselt (1948) had groups of professional weight lifters and watchmakers judge the same series of twelve weights to determine whether their contrasting experiences, and thus their different reference scales formed outside the laboratory, would affect their judgments. While both groups of subjects developed categories corresponding to the relative positions of the series stimuli, the weight lifters placed heavier weights in the "medium" categories than the watchmakers did, thus revealing the effects of their reference scales previously established in occupational experience with much heavier weights.

In experiments studying the formation of a judgment scale, stimuli are usually presented repeatedly in random order. The result is a well-practiced and fairly stable scale conforming on the whole to the position of the stimuli. However, this procedure tends to cancel out effects of the *order* and *frequency* of presentation, which are not always random in real life. Some stimuli are encountered more frequently than others, like the heavy weights by the weight lifters. The

segment of stimulus values experienced with greater frequency thus produces an effect like an anchor stimulus, but
in this case the anchor is an internalized concept of weight.

Acquisition of values through learning. The preceding
studies have dealt primarily with the influence of past experience in the placement of stimuli. A related problem concerns the role of experience in determining the affective
value of stimuli. Certain social categories come to denote a
range of positive values and others a negative evaluation.
How does the individual acquire values for these categories
and how does internalization of their values affect his placements?

One of the early studies of the acquisition of value categories was undertaken by Proshansky and Murphy (1942),
who proceeded on the assumption that rewards or reinforcements provided by other people represent a model for attack-
ing the general problem. They used the extent of lines as the
dimension of judgment, deliberately providing a margin for
error by presenting stimuli in a semidark room. In a pre-
training session, subjects estimated the lengths of lines, some
of which were "long" (5–7 inches), some "short" (2–4 inches),
and some "intermediate" with lengths between 4–5 inches
and thus overlapping somewhat with the "short" range. During a training period, each time a "long" line was presented
the subject received 15 cents, and each time a "short" line
was presented he had to forfeit 15 cents. In the final testing
period, the subjects judged the "intermediate" lines without
rewards or forfeits. Comparison of the final judgments of the
"intermediate" lines with those made prior to the rewards
showed a systematic shift toward greater length, that is, in
the rewarded direction. Judgments of control subjects who
were not rewarded or punished did not shift significantly.

These results were obtained for judgments of stimuli with
small objective differences presented under low illumination.

Much smaller effects, if any, would be expected in judgments of a well-graded series under optimal conditions. However, Tajfel (1957) has reported that the judgment scale was expanded when the lightest and heaviest weights were rewarded, in comparison with conditions of no reward or indiscriminate reward for the various weights. His conclusion suggests an intensified "end anchoring" produced by rewarding the end categories.

The acquisition of value and its effect on judgment of a structured stimulus were demonstrated by Lambert et al. (1949) using preschool children as subjects. After repeated experiences of using chips to obtain candy from a slot machine, the children were presented with the task of reproducing the size of similar chips by adjusting a patch of light. A systematic error in the direction of overestimating the size of the valued chip was obtained. The direction of the error is probably a function of the close association of size and value concepts for very young children, to whom the "biggest" is usually also the "best." This association of value and size dimensions also prevails for certain classes of objects in the adult social world, and the value categories have been shown to affect size estimates of coins and of cards inscribed with different sums of money when no standard stimulus was immediately available (e.g. Bruner and Rodrigues, 1953; Carter and Schooler, 1949; Dukes and Bevan, 1952).

The definitive role of reward in producing the value concept and the anchoring effects was subsequently demonstrated by the Lamberts (1953) by comparing estimates of the token chips, which obtained the reward, with estimates of chips which were used merely to obtain more token chips. In this case, only the token chips were overestimated.

In each of the above experiments, value was attached to certain categories by rewarding their use; then the use of these categories was observed in the absence of reward. The effects on judgment were thus produced by internalized value concepts or anchors. Since the dimension judged was in every case measurable in physical units, it was possible to use systematic displacements as indicators of the internalized anchor.

Acquisition of values in social situations. Many social categories pertain to dimensions which are not defined primarily by well-graded physical differences. This is one reason why social psychologists have investigated the internalization of reference scales and anchors in judgment of unstructured or ambiguous dimensions. This topic was already introduced in Chapter 2 in connection with the formation of psychophysical and psychosocial scales. In the formation of psychophysical scales, gradations of external stimuli are the major factors, while in the shaping of psychosocial scales the major determinants are the social factors in the situation. Thus, in Sherif's experiments (1936, 1937), judgments of autokinetic movement were obtained in an individual session following exposure to the judgments of other individuals. The common range and norm established in the social situation were maintained when the subjects made judgments alone. This comparison is a commonly accepted procedure for determining whether or not a social standard has been internalized (e.g. Festinger, 1953). The internalized standard and range have been shown to persist for considerable periods, even as long as a year following exposure to the social standard.

These findings are to be compared with those reported by the Luchins (1955) and Asch (1956) for judgments of discriminable differences in length when the social standard contradicted the perceived differences. Both report a sharp reduction in error, almost to the vanishing point, when individuals exposed to social standards which contradict their own perceptions subsequently give their judgments silently or alone. In social life, a completely arbitrary social definition of clearly apparent stimulus differences, as used in the Luchins and Asch experiments, is decidedly unusual. Arbitrary categorizations are offered when the stimulus situation provides several alternatives.

In an unstructured situation it has been found that a judgment range provided by a plant is effective even when the naive subject does not start making judgments aloud until the plant has withdrawn from the situation. An autokinetic experiment by Hood and Sherif (1961) was designed to minimize factors which might lead the subject to distort his judgments deliberately just to appear agreeable or nondeviant and which might lead him to suspect that the study was related to "social influence." The prescribed judgments of another person were introduced briefly, and apparently coincidentally, before the subject participated in the task. The plant was removed before the naive subject made judgments. Thus the subject did not commit himself relative to the plant's judgments and he was encouraged to make judgments as he saw fit. Two different prescribed ranges were employed. For each range, it was demonstrated that the subjects' judgments were concentrated significantly within the prescribed range to which they had been exposed briefly prior to rendering judgments. Questionnaire results indicated that subjects accepted the situation as it was presented to them and were largely unaware of the extent to which their judgments had been influenced. In an unstructured situation allowing response alternatives, the individual assimilates a social anchor, provided it does not conflict markedly with a range and mode of judgment he has formed previously, and his spoken judgments are indicative of this fact.

A common procedure for studying reinforcement in unstructured situations has been for the experimenter to tell the subject that he is "right" or "wrong" on given trials. Coming from the experimenter who arranged the procedures, such reinforcement can be regarded as more "authoritative" than the spoken judgments of another subject. Apparently the scheduling of verbal reinforcements and the manner of their cessation by the experimenter affect the outcome. Spivak and Papajohn (1957) affirmed certain judgments by calling them "right" either on a "variable interval" schedule ("partial reinforcement") or on a regular schedule. When, after a total of twenty "correct" responses under each schedule during the training period, the experimenter suddenly stopped saying "right," subjects trained on the variable interval schedule continued for eighty trials to give estimates within the range previously called right. This quite persistent maintenance of a range in the absence of affirmation by the experimenter would indicate that it had been internalized. On the other hand, subjects who had regularly received affirmation during training did not respond in a predictable direction following cessation of the reinforcement. Variability of judgment and percentage of formerly "incorrect" responses increased rapidly, the direction of change being toward increased judgment values in some cases and decreased values in others.

In Kelman's study (1950), instructions to the subject that most of his judgments were correct produced more stable responses than instructions that most of his judgments were incorrect. The latter instruction made the subject more susceptible to another social influence—the judgments of a partner. These findings were substantiated by Mausner (1954a), who reported that once the subject internalizes a standard reinforced as correct by the experimenter, he may respond to a plant whose judgments differ from his own by further emphasizing the difference between them. His judgments move further *away* from those of the plant, which is a contrast effect.

In social interaction, the individual faces different types

and sources of rewarding circumstances. While the reference scale and standard internalized as a result of reinforcements from one source may be predicted, it does not follow that the result of reinforcements from several sources is an algebraic sum of their single effects. It is possible that a more elaborate conception of the nature of social reinforcements and their interaction is required. Mausner and Bloch (1957) introduced variations in three different reinforcing circumstances: success in a judgment task prior to the experiment proper, the partner's success, and prior cooperative experiences in working on another task. The joint action of the three variables produced the largest judgment shifts in predicted directions—toward or away from a partner's judgments. However, when the variables operated in conflicting directions, in terms of previous experimental evidence of their effectiveness, prediction of the shift in individual judgments became extremely difficult.

This finding is consonant with Walter's conclusion (1955) that conflicts of social anchorages produce large increases in individual differences in judgment. Mausner and Bloch conclude that the interaction of variables may not be an additive process in the sense implied by concepts of "resultants of forces."

The Individual's Stand as an Internal Anchor

Regardless of the definition of "attitude" preferred by different authors, the data from which attitude is inferred are judgmental reactions by an individual. An attitude implies a characteristic and consistent mode of behavior toward its objects. Arousal of an established attitude brings greater consistency to judgments of different dimensions. The consistency in judgments of different dimensions can be understood in terms of the persistence of the attitudinal anchor from one task to the next.

Asch, Bloch, and Hertzman noted that "judgments made

in response to different aspects of the same situation became related to each other" (1938, p. 251). The relationship between judgments in different dimensions was higher when the object of judgment was also the object of an established attitude than when it was not. Thus, mean correlations between judgments of different personal characteristics from photographs of strangers were substantially lower than between judgments of different dimensions for occupations or well-known political figures.

The characteristic relatedness of judgments pertaining to objects of established attitudes was demonstrated some twenty years ago for predictions of future events. The future, of course, is seldom completely determinate, particularly the distant future. Studies by McGregor (1938) and Cantril (1938) show that in making predictions of more indeterminate and distant future events, the individual's attitude is a particularly potent anchor for his judgments. An attitude toward a political movement, for example, is reflected in the individual's judgments of specific events that would affect that movement (Cantril, 1938, p. 387). Persons with strong attitudes toward sociopolitical trends make judgments about the future with greater certainty, and their predictions resemble those made by other individuals with similar attitudes. On the other hand, persons who do not have definite attitudes toward the issue in question are less certain of their judgments (p. 388) and their judgments differ considerably from each other (McGregor, 1938, p. 183).

The persistent use of an established stand as an anchor for judgments of different aspects of stimuli was demonstrated recently by Secord, Bevan, and Katz (1956). Photographs of unknown individuals were presented for judgment of ten physiognomic traits associated with "Negroidness" and fifteen personality characteristics associated with the prevailing stereotypes of Negroes. Some of the photographs were of

Negro and some of white individuals, the former representing "a considerable range of variation in Negroidness." The most significant finding was that judgments of personality characteristics (stereotypes) of photographs varying widely in physiognomic traits did not differ significantly. "That is, even if he has a Caucasian-like appearance, a Negro will be seen as having, in full degree, all the stereotyped traits usually attributed to the Negro [and] there is no decrease in stereotyping in moving from the most Negroid Negroes to the most Caucasian" (p. 82). A significant tendency was found for the more anti-Negro judges to "exaggerate the personality stereotype of Negroes" in comparison with judges labeled "neutral" or "pro-Negro" on the basis of test scores. Anti-Negro judges also tended to judge the physiognomic traits as more Negroid than other judges. The individual's stand toward Negroes provided a common anchor for judgments of different characteristics.

Additional illustrations of the effect of the individual's own stand on his evaluations are furnished by experiments on the influence of attitudes toward various groups on the evaluation of performance. One of the pioneer studies of this type was by Chapman and Volkmann (1939) on estimation of future performance. College students were presented a literary information test with fifty multiple-choice items. One alternative was correct for each item. All subjects were informed that the maximum score was fifty and were shown sample items. Prior to the test, each subject was asked to write the score he expected to make. Three groups of subjects were also given information concerning the average score made by other groups on the test. A control group did not receive such information. The score attributed to other groups was the same in every case (37.2), but it was attributed to literary critics in one group, to college students like the subjects in another, and to day laborers in the third. It is to be stressed that no mention was made in the instructions of the social position of these three groups relative to the subjects. As in Perloe's study (1960) mentioned earlier, the standing of one's own group became an internal anchor for comparisons involving others.

The results were clear and significant. The average expected performance for the control group was 26.95; for the group receiving the scores of experts, it was 23.09; and for the group receiving the score of a group presumably inferior in this kind of task, it was 33.05. These variations in estimate of expected performance are in terms of the standing of the subjects' group relative to the other groups in this task. Relative to experts, the subjects' group stands low, hence a lowered prediction of own performance. Relative to day laborers, the subjects' group stands high, hence an increased prediction. The position of one's own group serves as an anchor determining the direction of the variations in estimates.

Interested by the finding that none of the subject groups estimated their performance as high as the fictitious scores of other groups, Hansche and Gilchrist (1956) conducted a similar experiment varying the level of score attributed to other groups and the difficulty of the task, as well as the relative positions of groups whose supposed performance was presented. Subjects were undergraduates in a psychology course and the tests were on general knowledge of psychology.

Significant effects were obtained for each of the three variables. Expected scores were set above the attributed performance of a lower group (high school seniors) and below that of a higher group (first-year graduate students) for two of the three levels of performance (percentage scores of 54.4 and 69.4). In no case did the mean expected score exceed the highest attributed level of performance (84.4), a level apparently more comparable to that used by Chapman and

Volkmann. However, in the most difficult test, the subjects rejected the high performance level when attributed to high school seniors and based their estimates on task difficulty.

The over-all conclusion that can be drawn is that within a wide range subjects adjust their estimates of future performance in terms of the position of their own group relative to others, in line with Chapman and Volkmann's findings. In doing so, they are also affected by the absolute level of performance attributed to other groups in terms of the difficulty of the task.

It is readily apparent that one's performance on a task arouses attitudes concerning his capabilities and personal worth relative to others and that these are issues which are highly charged motivationally and affectively. But the anchoring effects of attitudes are not unique to self-judgments. In several experiments, a close relationship has been found between variations in judgment of another person's performance and the social standing of the performer. High and significant correlations were obtained between estimates of future performance by a fellow member of one's group and that member's status in the group (Harvey, 1953). When performance level cannot be precisely determined by the subject, similar systematic variations obtain in one's judgments of completed performance by other members of his group (Sherif, White, and Harvey, 1955). The direction of displacements is toward overestimating performance by members with high status and underestimating performance by members with low status.

The high correlations between direction of the systematic variations in judgment and independent measures of the status of the performer mean that the judges use a common standard for judgment, deriving from their expectations for a person with a high or a low status in their group, as the case may be.

In two experiments, one using members of experimentally formed groups and one using members of friendship groups established in real life, systematic errors were found in judgments of performance by members of one's own group and by members of an antagonistic or disliked group (Harvey, 1956; Sherif et al., 1956). In the presence of a disliked group, individuals place the performance of members of their own group at a higher level than the performance of the deprecated out-group. One's stand toward his own group relative to the disliked out-group serve as anchors for his judgments and result in systematic displacements, even though the subjects were instructed simply to judge the performance they had witnessed. The task of judging the performance of another person who had an established relationship to oneself and one's group situationally aroused relevant attitudes. In the absence of unequivocal external standards of performance, these affective-motivational factors became the chief determinants of the level of placement.

Presentation of stimuli for judgments that pertain to significant social issues brings affective and motivational factors into the judgment process. Through prior experience with social objects and persons, the individual has formed attitudes defining his stand in the available range of categories and placing other stimulus items accordingly. He is highly partial to items placed in his own stand and antagonistic toward items placed in other categories. His attitude on the particular issue defines his own position relative to significant aspects of his social environment. When he is asked to appraise relevant stimuli, he may become as personally involved as though his own worth were called into question. The anchoring of judgment by an established attitude is an instance of ego-involvement. It is revealed in systematic variations in judgment when stimulus arrangements permit alternative placements.

Conditions in Which Social Anchors Are Effective

Every human group possesses a body of categories and ranks for the placement of persons and their behavior, other groups, and social objects. A noteworthy feature of social categorizations is their definition of the desirable, the expected, and even the ideal range of behavior, of position, of aspiration for members of the group. The opposites are specified or implied. When different individuals judge socially relevant dimensions, the social origins of their categories are revealed in their placements.

Let us take judgment of dimensions of the human figure as an example. In comparison with estimates of the size of cards, judgments of height of human figures by different individuals are in greater agreement (Parducci, 1954). Such judgments are frequently made and the range of ordinary dimensions in a human society is well known. In addition, however, society defines a range of desirable proportions for the male and female figure. Thus judgments of body dimensions by women reflect the social norms of an idealized figure as well as knowledge of actual proportions (Jourard and Secord, 1955).

The new member of a group faces value concepts or social norms as external stimuli. Specific manifestations of these social categories are encountered frequently in significant situations. These specific manifestations include the behavior of other individuals—their deeds, their expressions, and their words—as well as written language. Since contact with stimuli is a necessary first step in learning, reactions to external social standards have implications for the learning process through which social categories are internalized. Experiments introducing social categories or standards have resulted in considerable knowledge about the conditions in which contact with social categories effectively influences the

individual's judgments. The effect of a social standard introduced by the experimenter can be treated as a reaction to an
external anchor, as we have seen. Here we are interested in
reactions to social anchors for purposes of clarifying the conditions in which they are internalized.

To establish a clear baseline, we start with a simple laboratory demonstration by Reese, Volkmann, and their associates
(1953). When judgments were made of numbers of dots so
large that the subject could not estimate accurately, the experimenter's comment that "most people tend to overestimate" resulted in the subject's underestimating. When the
experimenter said that "most people tend to underestimate,"
the subjects overestimated. However, when the number of
items was easily perceptible during their exposure, say six
items or less, the experimenter's comments had no effect
upon judgment at all. This finding illustrates a general conclusion from experiments on reactions to social anchors:
When the stimulus dimension being judged permits response
alternatives, social standards provided by other people influence placement; however, when the stimulus dimension
is well structured or unequivocal, the effect of social standards is minimal.

A social standard introduced in a stimulus situation
which lacks a graded series of items, an objective standard,
and means of validating the correctness of judgment is likely
to be highly effective. When making judgments in such a
situation, the individual experiences considerable uncertainty. The judgments of another person may be the only external criteria available to him. If two naive individuals
make judgments which differ considerably, their uncertainty
is increased. Over a series of trials, their judgments converge toward each other. If, however, one individual is instructed to maintain a mode and range of judgment prescribed by the experimenter, the judgments of the single

naive subject move toward that prescribed mode and range. This, very briefly, is the finding in a number of experiments utilizing stimulus arrangements like the autokinetic situation or increasing the response alternatives by brief exposure times and/or small stimulus differences (e.g. Bovard, 1948; McCord, 1948; Sherif, 1936, 1937; Sinha, 1952).

Coffin (1941) introduced "incorrect" directions on the dials which subjects turned to adjust a comparison tone "equal" to a presented standard stimulus. Variations in stimulus structure were introduced by selecting tonal attributes for which discrimination is relatively easy (pitch), relatively difficult (volume), and impossible because the attribute ("orthosonority") is fictitious. The findings concerning the relative effect of the directions on judgments in these three conditions are clear: "high pitch is most resistant to suggestion, low pitch next so; volume is almost completely 'suggestible,' and orthosonority is consistently suggestible in either . . . direction. The relative 'suggestibility' of these attributes thus increases directly with increasing degrees of attributive 'ambiguity,' when ambiguity is judged in terms of evidence marshalled from the literature and from the present experiment" (p. 109).

Further confirmation of the differential effects of social standards in stimulus situations of varying structure comes from experiments on judgment of length of lines by Luchins (1944, 1955) and Asch (1952, 1956). The Luchins conclude: "The experimenter's decision was influential in getting subjects to accept or reject any proffered structurization of the line for the ambiguous perceptual stimuli but . . . it was very ineffective in producing any deviations from objectively true judgments when nonambiguous stimuli were employed" (Luchins, 1955, p. 297). Likewise, Asch's findings when standard lines were presented with an unequal comparison are quite clear. The percentage of error in the direction of erroneous judgments by planted subjects decreased regularly as the discrepancy between standard and comparison rose from .25 inches to .50 and .75 inches. In Asch's words, "the frequency of errors varied inversely with the magnitude of discrepancy" (Asch, 1956, p. 61).

An experiment by J. D. Thrasher (1954) varied both the margin for error in stimulus arrangements and the source of a social anchorage. The social anchor in this experiment was the spoken judgment of another person—in some cases a stranger and in others a close friend. Judgments were made of the location of stimulus lights randomly scattered on the face of a circular backdrop. In three experimental conditions, different portions of the circular backboard were illuminated with phosphorescent lucite in a dark room. The location and number of these luminous anchoring points were varied as follows. In condition A a complete circle of lucite bound the circumference of the board. In condition B, only two small segments of the circumference were visible, but a third indicating the center of the circle was presented before initial judgments were made. In condition C, the least structured situation, five points of lucite evenly spaced along the radius from the center to the circumference were presented prior to the judging and were removed while judgments were made.

When subjects judged the location of lights one by one with the physical anchors available in the three conditions, the mean error in condition B was almost double that of condition A with the full circle visible, and average error in the least structured condition was almost double that of condition B. Individual differences in error were greatest in the least structured condition, least in the most structured condition, and intermediate for condition B.

Subsequently, when pairs of close friends and pairs of

strangers made judgments in the three stimulus conditions, it was found that the relative effectiveness of the judgments of a friend or a stranger did not differ significantly in the most structured condition, but did differ significantly in both the intermediate (B) and least structured (C) condition. The trend of shifts in the least structured situation was toward agreement with the partner's judgments, particularly if the partner was a friend. We may conclude that as the stimulus arrangements become less structured, the margin for error increases and the spoken judgments of another person are more effective. The known difference in social relationships with the other person was revealed only in the less structured conditions.

As Thrasher's findings indicate, a second major factor determining the effectiveness of social anchors is their *source*. On a simplified level, Mausner (1953, 1954b) demonstrated that assimilation to a partner's judgments was greater when the partner had been previously seen to "succeed" in another task than when he had "failed." Heightened confidence in another's judgments is presumably an elementary basis for the superior effect of standards from experts (Moore, 1921) or "authoritative" sources (Asch, 1940). However, a given level of confidence in another's judgments is itself a product of placing the source in a category on one's reference scale of superiority-inferiority in, say, knowledge of the stimulus material and task. A judgment of the source underlies its influence or lack of it. Placement is not always made solely in terms of the source's knowledge. The source's relationship to oneself and one's group is also involved, and this relationship may vary considerably in terms of its motivational and affective components. That is why in some matters an authoritative or expert standard may be less effective than a standard from one's peers or one's parents. For example, college students' judgments of language usage were not affected as much by standards attributed to an expert in language as by those attributed to other students (Moore, 1921).

The placement of the source in a series in which oneself occupies a position is also important in determining the effects of standards presented by a "majority." The relative effectiveness of a "majority" is determined to an important degree by the individual's relationship to the source and his attitude toward the majority in question. Standards attributed to a congenial group (one's reference group) are more effective than those attributed to an out-group, which are usually rejected altogether if the out-group is placed low on one's preference scale (Asch, 1940). The majority of a group of which one is a member ordinarily affects his judgments more than a majority of persons assembled casually in the laboratory (Bovard, 1953; Deutsch and Gerard, 1955). Within one's own group, the influence of various members on judgment varies in terms of their status and power in the group organization. The initial presentation of judgments by high status members produces a less heterogeneous judgment scale than random presentation of judgments by members throughout the power structure (Zeller, 1955).

The relatively greater effectiveness of social standards attributed to one's group and to members with high status is one key to the establishment of internalized anchors. Socialization consists in large part of the individual's becoming related psychologically to small and large groups of which he is a member or aspires to be a member. The adoption of such "reference groups" is effected through an internalization process whereby the individual learns and accepts their value categories or norms and status system as his own. Henceforth, the individual's behavior relative to many social objects and persons is regulated to a considerable extent by the norms and status relations of his reference groups. The literature on reference groups (e.g. Sherif, 1948; Shibutani, 1955) reveals that various attitudes of an individual can be predicted from knowledge of his major reference groups and their value systems.

INTERACTION OF SCALES AND ANCHORS

In this chapter the effects of internal anchors have been emphasized. However, the intent of this emphasis is not to obscure the importance of other factors in judgment. In judgments of complex social stimuli, reference scales and internal and external anchors may interact in rather complicated fashion. The joint determination of judgment by several anchors is probably typical in the social area.

A classic example of reciprocal effects of a value scale, objective anchors, and internal anchors is Marks' study (1943) of skin-color ratings by Negro students. Marks studied the relations between ratings of skin color and ratings of attractiveness, and the relation between the judge's own skin color and his ratings of others in this respect. The dimensions of judgment were "very attractive—very unattractive" and "very dark—very light."

Certain of Marks' predictions were based on observations by the sociologist C. S. Johnson that the reference scale for skin color among Negro youth at the time placed a very dark color at the unfavorable end and a light brown at the favorable end. In line with Johnson's observations, Marks found "a tendency to displace the ratings of subjects considered attractive in the direction of the preferred skin color, a given subject being placed nearer this color by raters who consider her attractive than by those who consider her unattractive" (p. 376).

By means of a matching technique, Marks was able to obtain independent measures of objective skin color. In rating the skin color of others, the judge's own skin color served as anchor in addition to the most preferred color. The individual judge was not entirely objective about his place on the scale. The tendency was to displace one's own color toward a more moderate color. For individuals at both extremes—very light and very dark—this displacement was in the direction of the preferred light brown. However, it is of highest theoretical importance that the objective series of skin colors did influence judgments. The objective position of a person was reflected in the finding that individuals did not displace their own color to the opposite end of the continuum, but shifted their position and judged the relative location of others using their own skin color as a standard. Other individuals were rated light and dark in terms of one's own skin color. Thus a given individual might be rated differently by two different judges, yet his relative position was similar. If he were very dark, he would not be judged as very light.

Quite similar trends were obtained in a more recent study by Hinckley and Rethlingshafer (1951) on judgments of heights of men. These investigators concluded that "the judgment of the average height of all men is influenced by the height of the man making the judgment. The 'meaning' of the social value terms of 'short' and 'tall' is in part determined by the height of the judge" (p. 262). Displacements in judgment produced by the differences in internal standards were not, however, found to the same extent in judging all heights. Stimulus determinants were also operative. Thus the influence of one's own height as a standard is "controlled by the objective facts, particularly in judging the extreme heights" (p. 262). The extreme heights also serve as anchors for judgment, the variations caused by differing conceptions of medium height exerting their chief effects on judgments of heights between the extremes.

METHODOLOGICAL REMARKS: ATTITUDES STUDIED THROUGH JUDGMENTAL VARIATIONS

In much recent research, systematic variations of judgment are used as indicators of the influence of attitudes and other motives. Under some circumstances, motivational factors produce systematic displacements; under other circumstances, their operation increases the effectiveness of stimulus determinants, with the result that categorization is appropriate and variations in judgment are reduced. Evaluation of experimental findings, using displacement as an indicator of attitude functioning, requires analysis of the experimental circumstances, particularly the margin for displacement in the stimulus arrangements.

The margin for systematic displacements is minimal when each of a series of objects, varying on a discriminable dimension, is presented for comparison with another object. For example, in the method of constant stimuli, each stimulus is preceded or followed by an explicit standard. In the paired-comparison method, two items of the series are presented simultaneously and the subject has only to choose one of them as the "greater," "more favorable," "more pleasant," etc.

With no explicit standard designated by the experimenter, the margin for error is greater. The method of single stimuli dispenses with an explicit standard, as does the equal-interval procedure. The latter has much in common with the method of single stimuli; its chief difference is that a much larger number of items (usually verbal) are presented simultaneously for judgment. The larger number of items and simultaneous presentation constrain the subject to make judgments of one item at a time with occasional reference to prior placements.

At an opposite pole from a graded series of stimuli with an explicit standard lie stimulus arrangements which lack a graded series in dimensions defined by physical units and which provide no objective standard for judgment. Here the margin for systematic variation is maximal; several response alternatives are feasible.

Between these modal stimulus arrangements, all manner of variations in the compellingness of stimulus determinants is possible. Careful analysis of stimulus arrangements and procedures may be the first step in articulating different lines of experimentation for judgment of neutral objects and for "social judgment."

If the research problem concerns attitudes or other motives and uses systematic variations in judgment as behavioral indicators, an experimental situation permitting alternative placements is appropriate. The lack of objective standards when an object is judged from memory, for example, allows attitude to function as an anchor (Carter and Schooler, 1949). There are, of course, internal factors other than attitude which may anchor the judgment process. In their study of estimates of future performance, Chapman and Volkmann (1939) reported that when each subject knew his past performance in the task, systematic displacements produced by attitude were reduced to the point of insignificance. In effect, two internal standards were available—concepts of past performance and attitude—and knowledge of past performance was more directly relevant to the task of estimating future performance.

In judgments of verbal material, the effects of internal anchors other than attitude are reduced when unfamiliar material or ambiguous statements are presented. The results of "prestige suggestion" studies using literary passages, for example, attached to the names of authors toward whom subjects have differing attitudes probably depend on both conditions (Das et al., 1955). If subjects were familiar with the passages, they would doubtless make placements on the basis of their knowledge about them and their authors. A study by Moos and Koslin (1952) demonstrates that attitudes toward political figures affect judgments of statements attributed to them when these statements are ambiguous and subject to differing interpretations.

An additional requirement for the study of systematic variations in judgment produced by attitude is that the stimulus material and procedures be effective in arousing the attitude under study. Several research tasks are implied. Obviously one task is to ascertain that the individual has a particular attitude toward the class of objects being judged. This apparent truism becomes especially important in studies of judgment using objects with social value; it has sometimes been assumed that the social value guarantees a particular stand toward the object on the part of the subjects (cf. Klein et al., 1951; Rosenthal and Levi, 1950). In addition the dimension of judgment in which variations are studied must bear some relevance to the subject's attitude. For example, performance level is relevant to one's attitudes toward the performer. The size dimension is relevant to attitudes toward objects whose value and size are associated, e.g. coins (Bruner and Rodrigues, 1953), the human figure (Jourard and Secord, 1955), portions of food (Beams, 1954). But size of the object forming a background for a political symbol is not particularly relevant to one's attitude toward the symbol (Klein, Schlesinger, and Meister, 1951), nor is the weight of books especially relevant to a person's attitude toward their contents.

Finally, when motives are the main variables being studied, a research problem is faced which is seldom encountered in studying placement of neutral items. Procedures or instructions which make the subject aware that his attitudes are being studied may arouse counter-motivations. This problem can be illustrated by Hammond's findings in a study of systematic error in judging verbal alternatives (Hammond, 1948). Verbal items with two alternative answers, both of them objectively wrong, were arranged in the form of an "information test." Items with factual alternatives were also included to make the test appear plausible to the subjects. One "test" dealt with labor matters and one with Russia. They were given to a group of businessmen and a group of men employed by a labor union. Hammond's prediction was that the errors made by subjects in these two groups on items with two "indeterminable" alternatives would take systematic directions predictable from the individual's attitudes toward labor and toward Russia. Significant differences in error in the predicted directions were obtained: a positive systematic error for one group as against a negative systematic error for the other. These results were supported in a study by Kubany (1953) using an entirely different issue. In short, when other internal anchors, such as knowledge of the facts, cannot be used in making a choice, one's attitude on the issue determines the outcome.

However, Hammond found that the influence of attitude in determining the direction of error could be vitiated by the simple device of labeling the test forms with the abbreviation "Att-Info-form." The abbreviation "Att" apparently indicated to subjects that their attitudes were being studied, and this awareness put them on guard lest their attitudes determine their choices.

The foregoing methodological remarks were made to clarify optimal experimental conditions for studying attitudes through judgmental indices. In brief, the optimal circumstances permit alternatives for response, reduce the availability of other standards (internal or external), effectively arouse the attitude being studied, and minimize the possibility of the subject's becoming aware that his behavior is being studied to learn something about his acceptance or rejection of the stimulus material.

PART TWO

Studies of Attitudes and Communication Effects

CHAPTER 5

Placement of Items on Controversial Social Issues

STIMULUS ITEMS which vary on a physical dimension can be placed relative to one another on the basis of differences that are measurable in commonly acceptable standards and units. Standards for ordering social stimulus items, on the other hand, differ in different historical periods, in different societies, and even between different groups within a single society. The differences between ordering items on physical and social dimensions need not imply, however, that one is more real than the other. For example, the fact that the value scales of different periods and different societies produce striking contrasts in the conduct and the aspirations of individuals is evidence of their reality.

When items pertain to a highly controversial social issue, the social dimension is ordinarily defined by the stands adopted by different groups of individuals on that issue. Thus today, items concerning social segregation of Negroes in the United States can be ordered in terms of the stands taken by particular groups. At one extreme, we might find proponents of total segregation, reminiscent of an apartheid policy. At the other, we might encounter advocates of complete integration in all phases of social life. The stands taken by the more prominent and larger groups today might be ordered between these extremes. At an earlier period, the one extreme was defined by the proponents of slavery and the other by the Abolitionists.

The extreme positions on a social issue are rather readily recognized by interested members of a society in a given period, and there is little error in placing expressions of the extreme views in appropriate end categories. In this chapter, we are concerned chiefly with placement of those items on a controversial social issue which lie between the extremes defined by current social realities. Experiments are summarized dealing with the placement of such items by individuals maintaining different stands on the issue.

Proponents of a particular stand on a controversial social issue are not ordinarily neutral toward stimulus material concerning that issue. Just as the task of predicting one's own performance in an important activity has motivational significance, so the task of judging items on a social issue involves the attitudes of the individual who strongly supports a particular stand on that issue as his own stand. The presentation of items pertaining to the issue serves in itself to arouse his established attitudes, thereby involving them in the judgment process. The relationship between the individual and the stimulus material is an ego-involved relationship.

How then does the individual order items on a highly ego-involving issue? Does he employ standards and categories common to all individuals in his society at the time, regardless of their stands on the issue? Or is placement of the items affected by the internal anchors and categories provided by his attitudes? In the preceding chapter, several representative experiments were summarized which demonstrated systematic variations in judgment, the direction of variation being determined by the individual's attitudes. The experiments in this chapter concern the problem of categorizing items on a controversial social issue by individuals upholding different stands on the issue.

Effect of Attitude on Placement of Items on Controversial Issues

Some years prior to most of the experiments summarized in the last chapter, L. L. Thurstone presented a rationale and method for measuring attitudes which initiated an extensive program to develop scales to assess attitudes toward numerous social issues. The rationale was based on his "law of comparative judgment" and was jointly inspired by psychophysical research and normal probability statistics. Thurstone offered a rational basis for quantifying psychological scales in areas which cannot be related to independently measurable physical dimensions such as weight, pitch, or inclination.

One major procedure in the preparation of a Thurstone scale is placement by judges of a considerable number of statements from which final items for the scale are selected. On the basis of the judges' sortings, scale values for the statements are obtained and final selection of test items is made. The most widely used procedure has been the method of equal-appearing intervals, since the large number of statements to be judged makes other methods (e.g. paired comparisons) time-consuming and laborious.

In the present context, our interest is not in the utility of Thurstone attitude scales or other attitude measurement techniques, but in judgments of verbal statements under the equal-appearing intervals procedure. As noted in Chapter 2, stimulus arrangements in this procedure are less conducive to fine discriminations than, say, the method of paired comparisons or the ranking method, if in the latter method the number of items is not overly large. We might suspect, therefore, that the sorting of a large number of statements on a social issue using this procedure might be subject to systematic variations.

Thurstone's rationale for constructing an attitude scale required the assumption that scale values obtained from judges' sortings were independent of the judges' own stands on the issue. "If the scale is to be regarded as valid, the scale values of the statements should not be affected by the opinions of the people who help construct it. This may turn out to be a severe test in practice, but the scaling method must stand such a test before it can be accepted as being more than a description of the people who construct the scale" (Thurstone and Chave, 1929, p. 92).

The first special test of this assumption was made by Hinckley (1932) on sortings of 114 statements on the social position of Negroes by judges with pro-Negro and anti-Negro attitudes and by Negro judges. He reported that the average scale values for judges in the two white groups were highly correlated ($r = .98$) and that scale values for anti-Negro and Negro judges were also closely related. Similar findings were reported by Pintner and Forlano (1937) for sortings of statements on the Attitude toward Patriotism scale.

On the basis of supportive evidence from experiments, accounts of scaling methods in textbooks usually concluded that judgment of items by the method of equal-appearing intervals is unaffected by the attitudes of judges. At the same time there was increasing research evidence on the systematic variations in judgment produced by attitudes, as indicated in the previous chapter. As a result, an investigator in this area faced an uncomfortable paradox. Edwards and Kenney suggested in 1946 (p. 82) that available evidence was insufficient for a definitive conclusion.

A subsequent investigation by Eysenck and Crown on sortings of statements on anti-Semitism concluded that "the personal views of the judges did not influence their ratings" (1949, pp. 49–50). The forty anti-Semitic judges and forty "least anti-Semitic" judges in this study were selected by "giving them the Primary Social Attitudes questionnaire, and scoring them on the anti-Semitic questions contained in it," viz. two items (p. 54). The above conclusion was based on a "correlation between *average ranking* of the 150 items" which was .98. However, following the sortings, "all items showing disagreement among the judges with respect to scale position were discarded, and 24 items were finally retained" (p. 50).

The present authors suspected that, for one reason or another, research investigating the Thurstone assumption had not tested it under optimum conditions. For example, in the Eysenck and Crown study, there apparently were differences in scale position which were not examined. In the Pintner and Forlano study carried out in the thirties, the investigators were unable to secure any group that could be called unpatriotic, and there is some question as to the general level of personal involvement of the subjects with this issue at the time.

On the other hand, the issue in the Hinckley study, social position of Negroes, was surely ego-involving for the judges. Here a possible explanation for the high correlations obtained was the use of a procedure intended only to eliminate "careless" subjects. Hinckley observed that some subjects tended to bunch statements in one or more categories and to neglect others. "This phenomenon of bunching at the extremes was noticed in the case of certain of the white subjects, but was especially noticeable in the Negro subjects" (p. 283). Believing that this tendency resulted from poor discrimination and carelessness, the experimenter eliminated every case with 30 or more of the 114 statements in any one category.

On the hunch that this procedure to eliminate careless judges had unwittingly narrowed the range of attitudes by dropping the subjects most highly ego-involved in the issue, Hovland and Sherif (1952) undertook to replicate the Hinckley experiment, taking precautions to include subjects with highly ego-involved stands on the issue.

Judgment of Social Items with Equal-Appearing Intervals Procedure

In our experiment, the equal-appearing intervals procedure used by Thurstone and Chave (1929) and Hinckley (1932) was employed with the same instructions. A special point was made not to mention attitudes or attitude measurement in any way before the statements were sorted. The judging task was administered in relatively small groups under close supervision to insure uniform administration and to be sure that subjects understood instructions.

The set of 114 statements used by Hinckley represents a wide range of positions, with some clearly *pro* and others clearly *con* and with a large number of neutral or ambiguous items. The statements seemed suitable, therefore, to study placement of items between the extremes as affected by the ego-involvement of individuals with different stands on the issue. The literature on judgment cited in the last chapter clearly suggests the general hypothesis that the stand taken by an individual on an issue in which he is personally involved will constitute an anchor for his judgments, whether or not his attitude is specifically mentioned in the instructions.

The first two hypotheses pertained to the distribution of judgments in the eleven categories prescribed by the procedures (ranging from I, "most unfavorable in regard to the social position of Negroes," to XI, "most favorable in regard to the social position of Negroes"). Briefly, it was predicted that judges holding extremely favorable or unfavorable attitudes toward Negroes would concentrate their placements of the statements into a smaller number of the prescribed categories than would judges for whom the issue is less ego-involving, and that the bunching of items would tend to occur in the extreme categories. The latter prediction was based on the observation that individuals who are highly ego-involved in an issue are often quite discriminating in placing items in a category corresponding to their own stand on the issue, but lump together all statements differing from their own stand at the end of the scale they reject. These tendencies may be described as a *raised threshold of acceptance* and a *lowered threshold for rejection* on the part of highly ego-involved individuals.

Our final hypothesis pertained to the nature of items which would be subject to greatest displacement. In view of the manifold evidence demonstrating the keen discrimination of clear-cut stimulus differences, little if any displacement of clearly defined statements at the extremes was expected. However, on the basis of reports that neutral items are subject to differing interpretations, it was predicted that the greatest displacement of statements would occur in the neutral region. For example, Edwards (1946) reported that neutral items on Thurstone scales had larger interquartile ranges (Q values), and were more ambiguous and less differentiating than items at the extremes. He noted that the neutral region serves as a sort of catchall, including expressions of indifference and ambivalence. On all counts, one might anticipate displacement of such items by strongly involved subjects.

In order to assure the inclusion of individuals with varying personal involvement, subjects were chosen from groups known to have varied experiences pertinent to the issue. Of the 103 Negro subjects, 54 were students at the University of Oklahoma during the year following a Supreme Court decision ending segregation at the university. These more mature subjects had a sense of mission and more actual experience with discriminatory practices than the younger Negro subjects (N = 49) who were undergraduates at a state university for Negroes located in a Negro community.

In all, 194 white subjects were used, most of them unselected undergraduates in several different colleges and universities in Oklahoma and Georgia. Of these, a small group of 19 was composed of individuals who were known to have participated actively in antisegregation activities. Groups organized around an anti-Negro stand and comparable in age and educational level to other subjects were not available at the time of this study. It was necessary, therefore, to rely on responses to attitude statements administered *after* the sortings in order to select the most anti-Negro judges, and 17 subjects were chosen on this basis. It should be noted, however, that to the experimenters' knowledge these individuals, unlike the pro-Negro whites, had not engaged in any public or organized activity to advance their stand on the issue.

After the subjects had sorted the statements, procedures to secure further data on their attitudes were introduced. Subjects were instructed to select the pile (category) of statements which "comes closest to your view on the issue" and to write on that pile the word "agree," as well as one of the following to indicate the degree of their agreement: "very strongly," "strongly," or "mildly." Then they were instructed to select the pile "which is most objectionable from your point of view," to indicate their disagreement and its degree. This procedure seemed sufficient for checking the attitudes of Negro subjects. However, for white subjects, a further check on their attitudes was obtained by administering the Likert Negro Scale as the final step in the experiment. (This

form was not administered to Negro students because pre-
testing had revealed that they had a strong animosity toward
filling out a form prepared entirely from the white point of
view.)

Figure 8 shows the frequency distributions of statements
in the eleven categories for these subjects. In the top graphs,

Figure 8. Number of Statements Placed in Each of 11
Categories by Each Group of Judges

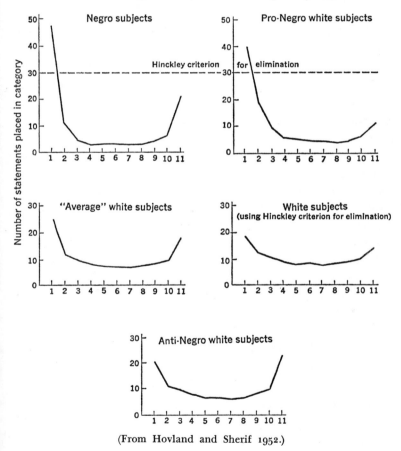

(From Hovland and Sherif 1952.)

the dotted line at 30 indicates the frequency in any one category which Hinckley used to eliminate subjects for carelessness. By this criterion, over three-fourths of the Negro and two-thirds of the pro-Negro white subjects would be eliminated from the analysis. It can be observed that frequencies in category I, the most unfavorable end, are markedly higher for Negro and pro-Negro subjects, who strongly disagree with the statements in this position. It may also be seen that the frequencies for the neutral categories are noticeably lower for these subjects than for the "average" or the anti-Negro white subjects.* However, when subjects who placed more than thirty statements in any one category are eliminated, a relatively flatter distribution results (lower right). The distribution for anti-Negro subjects is not strikingly different from average white subjects, although it shows a tendency to concentrate items at the favorable end of the scale.

In comparing scale values of the statements for the two groups, an effort was made to make as fair a test as possible by selecting statements equally appropriate for response by white and Negro subjects. (Some were clearly inappropriate for Negro subjects, e.g. "I would not patronize a hotel that accommodates Negroes.") It was possible to find eleven items which did not seem inappropriate for Negro subjects and which were approximately equidistant in the original Hinckley scaling (1930). The distributions of scale values for these items on the Hinckley attitude scale and those obtained from the sortings of our subject groups are given in Figure 9.

There is considerable similarity in the scale values for the average white subjects (with the Hinckley procedure of eliminating those with 30 or more statements in any cate-

* Throughout the remainder of the discussion of this study quotation marks will be omitted in referring to the "average" white subjects, but the reader will understand that the sample is not represented as a true random sample of white college students but only refers to the unselected subjects available where the study was conducted.

gory) and the scale values originally found by Hinckley. The correlation between the two sets of scale values for the eleven items is .96. But the scale values for the strongly pro-Negro white judges and for the Negro judges do not closely correspond to those obtained by Hinckley. In line with our

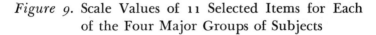

Figure 9. Scale Values of 11 Selected Items for Each of the Four Major Groups of Subjects

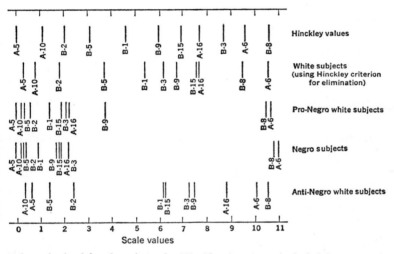

Values obtained for these items by Hinckley (1932) are included for comparison. (From Hovland and Sherif 1952.)

predictions, neutral items are displaced markedly toward the unfavorable end of the scale. While the rank order of the items for all groups is similar, the category placement differs markedly. The anti-Negro subjects also show a tendency to displace neutral items toward extreme categories, though not so markedly.

Can these findings be explained in terms of carelessness of the judges? In addition to procedural precautions taken to insure careful sorting, this possibility was checked by two means:

1. Without prior warning, subjects were asked after sort-

ing the statements to estimate the proportions of statements which were favorable and unfavorable to Negroes. Significant differences in the proper direction were obtained between estimates of the proportions of unfavorable statements by subjects who actually placed differing numbers of statements in the unfavorable categories.

2. In another part of this study, to be reported later in this chapter, the subjects were instructed to use any number of categories they thought necessary to distinguish among the items. The subjects who placed a large number of items in the extremes to the neglect of other categories when eleven categories were required also piled up statements in the extreme categories and used fewer categories when permitted to sort the statements into categories of their own choosing. These were the subjects with extreme stands on the issue, and displacements were largely of items in the neutral region. The displacements exhibited by extreme subjects cannot be attributed to their holding positions beyond the range used. All of the subjects readily selected one of the piles as representative of their own stand on the issue.

The differences between these findings and those of previous studies testing the assumption that attitudes do not influence judgments under equal-appearing intervals procedures seem to lie in the wider range of attitudes and stronger ego-involvement represented by our subjects and in the checks introduced to avoid eliminating these subjects for supposed carelessness.

Displacements under the Equal-Appearing Intervals Procedure

A general significance beyond mere demonstration of the effects of high ego-involvement with an extreme stand may be attached to the study summarized above. It corroborates considerable research evidence that procedures for the judgment of stimuli without an explicit standard (anchor) are conducive to systematic error produced by the different standards employed by the judges. As we observed in Chapter 3, systematic errors in judgment of a physical continuum occur when a series of items is presented without an explicit standard and when other stimuli with values beyond those of the series are repeatedly interpolated.

In judgment of verbal items, the margin for error is potentially great because language can be vague, ambiguous, and open to differing interpretations. However, the margin for error in judgment of verbal items is finite and not equal for all items. The statement "I detest bananas" is not ambiguous or vague and could be judged on a favorable-unfavorable continuum by anyone who knows the language. All statements are not so clear, however, particularly in the arena of social issues and social communication. When an item on a social issue is ambiguous, expresses ambivalence or indifference, judgments of it may vary as a function of the other statements judged, as well as in terms of individual standards.

Apparently for many social issues, extreme positions are more clearly stated and more easily recognized than the positions lying between the extremes. In our study just summarized, the extreme items were subject to less variation. Fehrer (1952) has demonstrated that elimination of items at one or the other extreme produces shifts in scale values for middle ("neutral") items adjacent to the "truncated" end of the series. In short, in judging verbal items under equal-intervals or single-stimuli procedures, the extreme end items have a functional significance affecting the placement of other items. Fehrer found that items in the neutral region, on the other hand, are subject to displacements and derive their functional significance from their relationship to the end positions.

When the individual judging items under these procedures is highly ego-involved in his position, his own stand functions as an anchor and neutral items are displaced systematically to the extent that they are ambiguous, ambivalent, and subject to alternative interpretations. Webb (1954) proposed a similar explanation of those irregularities in judgment under equal-interval procedures which he labeled "inversions."

If, however, simple statements of a fairly stereotyped and categorical nature are judged, displacements under equal-appearing intervals procedures would not be sufficient to affect scale values appreciably. Prothro (1955) used forty of the items from the Grice-Remmers "Generalized Scales to Measure Attitudes toward Any Group," which were constructed on the basis of "The Trait Book" of the Eugenics Record Office with a few statements adapted from Thurstone scales in highly generalized form. Arab judges in Lebanon, who were demonstrably ego-involved in their anti-Jewish positions, did displace these items to some extent, two of the forty items as much as two scale units. But displacements were not so marked as those by the highly involved subjects for the Negro issue in sorting statements which were by and large more complex and more subject to differing interpretations. The much smaller number of statements sorted under equal-intervals procedures by the Arab subjects was probably an additional condition favoring consistent placement.

Granneberg (1955) and Fishman and Lorge (1954) have reported displacements related to the judges' attitudes. Granneberg reported that analysis of the placements of particular items by selected groups of subjects suggests a rather complex interaction of attitude and intellectual factors producing displacement. Inasmuch as intelligence is related to comprehension of verbal items and instructions, such interaction is to be expected. Simple explanations in terms of high or low IQ's or educational achievement can hardly be expected to account completely for the interaction, as Granneberg implies. Certainly the intellectual accomplishments of the most involved Negro students and pro-Negro white students in our research were not inferior to those of most of our "average" white subjects; they exceeded them on the whole.

Likewise, a subject's ability to adopt and maintain the judging "set" specified in the instructions is a rather complex product of past experience, sophistication, educational achievement, intelligence, and ego-involvement. Webb (1954) observed fairly frequent instances of spontaneous changes in the dimension of judgment, from "favorable-unfavorable" to "agreement-disagreement." The "difficulty of maintaining a judging set" is not merely a function of the subject and the particular items he judges, however (Webb, 1955). Stimulus arrangements, as well as attitudinal and intellectual factors, are involved. The equal-intervals procedure, by presenting a large number of complex verbal statements for placement into a number of categories without explicit standards, presents a difficult task for the subject, thereby increasing the difficulty of categorizing items in terms of a prescribed dimension. The likelihood of falling back on the agreement-disagreement aspect is increased.

Recently Mausner (1960) reported that categorization of items on the Attitudes toward the Church Form (Thurstone and Chave) by the equal-appearing intervals procedures were significantly affected by the instruction: "Try to imagine that you are an extremely devout and faithful churchgoer as you are doing this. But remember that you are to rate the items, not your own feelings" (p. 2). These instructions produced "a piling up of responses at the extreme positions with a greater increase at the position at the end of the continuum opposite from the group's own stand" and significant shifts in mean ratings of a fourth of the items toward more extreme ratings, in line with the findings of the Hovland and Sherif study. These shifts are in comparison to a control group which sorted the items without the additional instruction. Interestingly enough, instructions to sort items as though "you are an atheist" produced no consistent trends, resulting instead in a striking increase in item variance. The results were clarified for Mausner when he found that all but two of his subjects were "faithful churchgoers" and that they expressed a complete lack of knowledge about an atheist stand. ("I haven't the faintest idea of what it feels like to be an atheist.") Mausner's results seem to indicate that dimensions of favorableness-unfavorableness and agreement-disagreement are rather intimately related and suggest that knowledge or familiarity about various positions probably interacts with these inevitably.

A Test by the Method of Paired Comparisons

Despite the precautions taken to check that the results of sorting items on the Negro issue were not due to carelessness, another difficulty remained: the piling up of items and neglect of certain categories were evidence that the judges could not discriminate the items in terms of favorableness to the social position of the Negro. A direct test of this possibility was made by Kelley, Hovland, Schwartz, and Abelson (1955) by presenting 20 of the 114 items to subjects from the same populations for judgment by the method of paired comparisons. This procedure presents only two statements at a time and requires that the subject choose one of the two as the more favorable.

Figure 10 shows a scatter diagram comparing scale values of items obtained by the method of equal-appearing intervals for Negro and white subjects. In comparison with Figure 11, which presents a scatter diagram of scale values obtained

for white and Negro subjects by the method of paired comparisons, it can be seen that most of the displacements in
scale values are eliminated in the paired-comparisons procedure. However, certain differences in scale values for the

Figure 10. Scatter Diagram of Scale Values Obtained
by the Method of Equal-Appearing Intervals

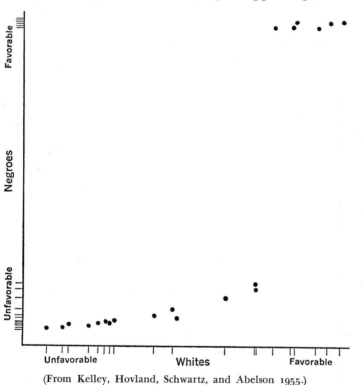

(From Kelley, Hovland, Schwartz, and Abelson 1955.)

two groups remain, including those circled in Figure 11.
Three of these were rated higher by white than by Negro
subjects, and one was rated higher by Negro subjects. The
former items express an ambivalent stand on the equality of
Negro and white groups.

Figure 12 is a scatter diagram of scale values for data obtained by equal-intervals procedures when computed by a
successive-intervals analysis. This statistical treatment is
based on the assumption of a normal distribution of placements for an item and is designed to yield "scale values that
are linearly related to those obtained by the method of
paired comparisons over the complete range" (Edwards,
1957, p. 122). It has been utilized previously to "correct"

Figure 11. Scatter Diagram of Scale Values Obtained
by the Method of Paired Comparisons for
White and Negro Subjects

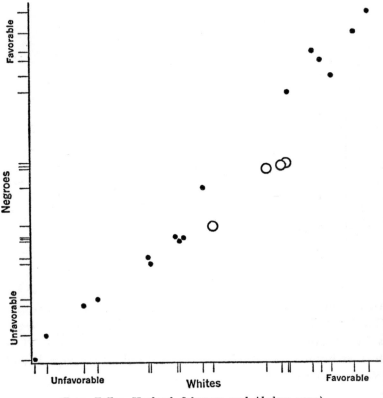

(From Kelley, Hovland, Schwartz, and Abelson 1955.)

for the curvilinear relationships of scale values obtained by these two methods at the ends of the scale. The result, as shown in Figure 12, is to bring the spacing of items for white

Figure 12. Scatter Diagram of Scale Values Obtained by the Method of Successive Intervals for White and Negro Subjects

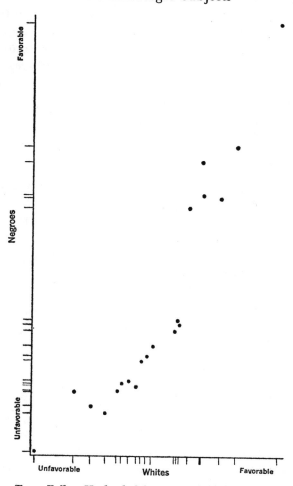

(From Kelley, Hovland, Schwartz, and Abelson 1955.)

and Negro subjects into closer correspondence, though not completely, by "stretching" the scale of Negro judges. Thus the range of category values is no longer equivalent for the two groups.

From this study, we may conclude that with stimulus arrangements and procedures making the judgment task more circumscribed and clear-cut, and forcing a choice between only two alternatives, the individuals could discriminate the items which by equal-appearing intervals procedures were subject to marked displacements. The paired-comparisons procedure forces the individual to recognize different stands on the issue, but does not require that he order them. The ordering is accomplished by the investigator through statistical analysis of the data.

Judgment of Items with Individual Choice of Categories—"Own" Categories

In making judgments in actual life, the number of categories employed is seldom prescribed by another person. Within the bounds of prevailing cultural and linguistic categories, the individual places items in any number of categories according to his preference. Of course he may be influenced by the number and type of categories used by others in his social milieu, but he is not ordinarily told to use, say, eleven or nine categories. In our study on the Negro issue, eleven categories ranging from "most unfavorable" to "most favorable" were imposed by the instructions. In spite of this, the frequency of actual use of the eleven categories differed for individuals upholding different stands on the issue. In a sense, the task of placing items is more natural and less artificial for the individual when he can define the number and size of the categories to be employed.

In accordance with our discussion of stimulus arrangements and procedures in the study of behavioral indicators of attitudes, it was reasonable to predict that displacement of items by subjects highly ego-involved with a stand would be even more accentuated if the number of categories was not fixed by experimental procedures (Sherif and Hovland, 1953). Accordingly, subjects were instructed to sort the same 114 statements on social position of Negroes into the number of categories they felt to be necessary. The instructions followed those used with eleven categories until the point at which the categories were specified. Then subjects were told:

> Write the number I on the top of the pile of cards which is most *unfavorable* regarding the social position of Negroes. Write II on top of the next pile. The *last pile* you number will be that pile of cards which is most favorable regarding the social position of Negroes.

One hundred and eighty-one subjects who served under the equal-appearing intervals procedure prescribing eleven categories also sorted the statements with these instructions. Most of these (151) sorted under the "imposed" category conditions two weeks prior to this experiment. The frequency distributions of number of categories used by subjects who had sorted first under the "imposed" and the distributions for those who first sorted under the "unrestricted" category conditions did not differ significantly. Additional subjects from the same population served only under the "unrestricted" or "own" category instructions.

When Negro and white subjects were instructed to choose the number of categories they deemed necessary, the more highly involved Negro subjects employed fewer categories than did the white judges. For example, a significantly greater proportion of Negro judges than white judges used four or fewer categories. Figure 13 gives the frequency distributions for placement of items by Negro subjects and white subjects using three and six categories. It may be ob-

served that regardless of number of categories used, the more
ego-involved Negro subjects piled up items at the "unfavorable" extreme.

> *Figure 13.* Distributions of Numbers of Statements
> Assigned to Each Category by Negro and
> White Judges Who Chose Either Three or
> Six as the Number of Categories Needed to
> Represent Differences among Statements
> concerning Social Position of Negroes

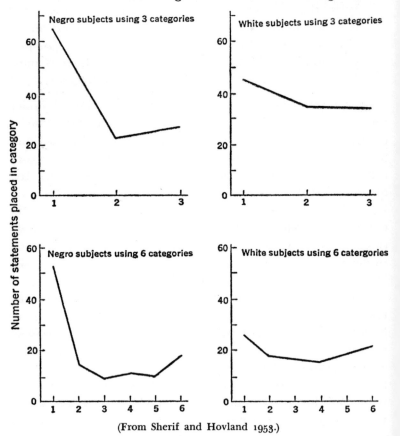

(From Sherif and Hovland 1953.)

When the sortings of those individuals who served under both imposed and unrestricted category conditions were compared, it was found that subjects who used fewer categories under the unrestricted conditions tended to be those who piled up statements under the imposed eleven-category procedure.

We were interested in the possibility of discovering a behavioral index of the individual's attitudes from the manner in which he sorted the items when not told how many categories to use. It was apparent on the basis of the above results that such an index would need to incorporate measures of the number of categories employed and of the tendency to concentrate judgments in extreme categories. To determine the feasibility of developing such an index in further research, an analysis of the five different types of subjects was made. The subjects included two Negro groups, one consisting of advanced students at a state university during the first year following desegregation, and the other a group of undergraduates at a Negro university. One small group of white subjects had actively participated in desegregation activities. Another small group was designated anti-Negro on the basis of answers to an attitude scale. Finally there was an unselected group of average white college students.

A two-item index was used summarizing constriction-extension of the individual's scale and extent of concentration on items at the anti-Negro end. The cutting point for constriction was between four and five categories. A cutting point for concentration of items in the extreme category was devised on the basis of chi-square analysis which permitted determination of the significance of concentration of judgments, taking into account the number of categories employed by an individual. Figure 14 gives the mean values thus obtained for the various subject populations. The groups are clearly differentiated on the basis of mean values; differences between the two Negro groups, between pro-Negro and anti-Negro whites, and between the less extreme Negro group and "average" white subjects are all significant at less than the 1 per cent level.

Figure 14. Mean Scale Scores (Based on Number of Categories Chosen and Skewness of Distributions) for Groups of Negro and White Judges Selected on Basis of Differences in Attitude Concerning Social Position of Negroes

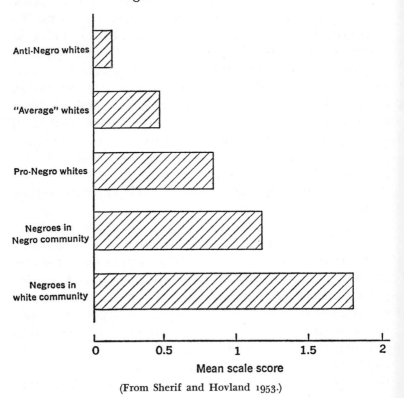

(From Sherif and Hovland 1953.)

It should be emphasized that the "constriction" variable referred to the number of categories used when the individual was allowed to determine any number that he saw fit, and *not* to the variance of individual judgments under instructions providing a prescribed number of categories. The finding by Manis (1960a) that the mean standard deviations of judgments on a 7-point scale by individuals who were profraternity and antifraternity were greater than the standard deviation for neutral subjects is in accord with the findings of our research. Had the same measure been employed for judgments of individuals with the prescribed category procedure in our research, it would have been greater for extremely pro- and anti-Negro subjects, who displaced many items to the extremes, than for unselected subjects, who distributed their judgments more evenly throughout the prescribed categories.

Since the index of constriction and concentration of items follows the predicted trend for Negro subjects newly arrived at a formerly segregated university, Negro subjects in a Negro university, and pro-Negro white subjects, the results can be attributed to the attitudinal variable without proposing cultural, educational, or intellectual factors peculiar to the Negro subjects. In a recent study by LaFave and Sherif (1959), the number of categories used in judging verbal items on the Negro issue differed significantly not only between Negro and white subjects but between anti-Negro white subjects and unselected white subjects, the anti-Negro white subjects using fewer categories than unselected subjects.

We may conclude that the relationship between the behavioral index and the criterion subject categories is sufficiently great to make this line of investigation a promising one. In judging social issues in actual life, the individual is frequently in a position to place items in terms of an unrestricted number of categories. Whether he does so in terms of simple dichotomous categories or whether he makes fine gradations in between may have considerable significance for his reactions to persons, groups, and events. It is possible that more accurate prediction of reactions, say, to a communication on an issue could be made if the individual's attitude were described by a behavioral index summarizing his characteristic discrimination of relevant items rather than by his responses to direct questions about his stand on the issue.

A related conception is offered by Mausner (1960) in connection with his experiment summarized earlier in this chapter. As noted, placements by individuals who were churchgoers were highly variable when they were instructed to assume the role of an atheist, but assumed a characteristic distribution when instructions told them to imagine they were devout churchgoers. Mausner suggests that the way individuals sort verbal statements might be

> an effective test of the ability of a group of people to assume a role [and] the degree to which subjects showed the Hovland and Sherif phenomenon when asked to act as judges in the construction of a Thurstone scale would indicate their success in assuming the role. This might be an invaluable independent check in an experimental situation in which the degree to which the subject identifies with a role is an important parameter of his behavior [p. 6].

MOTIVATION AND PLACEMENT OF CONTROVERSIAL SOCIAL ITEMS

Procedures in the foregoing experiment approximate more closely the setting in which social judgments are made than do the usual instructions prescribing a given number of categories. Therefore the results offer a glimpse of the manner

in which items on a controversial social issue are categorized
by individuals in actual life.

It was our hypothesis in these experiments that individuals
with established and definite stands on a controversial social
issue become ego-involved when they face the task of placing
items relevant to that stand, and that this ego-involvement
would affect their placements, the number of categories used,
and the relative frequency of their use. The rationale for this
prediction, which is supported by the results, is simple and
familiar. When an individual adopts a stand on a controversial issue, he is mindful of the prevailing opinions in the
groups of which he is a member or to which he aspires. Ordinarily his stand is harmonious with those of the groups to
which he is psychologically related. His stand is adopted
relative to the value scales of his reference groups (Sherif
and Sherif, 1953).

Attitudes related to reference group values are affect-laden,
and are functionally equivalent to that more general class of
variables called "social motives." These attitudes establish
a psychological relationship between the individual and his
social milieu, defining his position and stand on many issues
in social life, and his aspirations in the scheme of social life.
Thus they are constituents of a system of relationships which
delineate the individual's conception of himself (his "ego"
or "self"). This is one reason why changing such attitudes is
no small task and why a shift of reference groups is such an
effective way of accomplishing attitude change.

When faced with a task and material relevant to his established attitudes on a significant issue, the individual becomes
personally involved. Even though he is told to place items in
terms of their favorableness or unfavorableness on the issue,
his judgments are influenced by his own stand and by his
agreement or disagreement with the items. Thus the categories he uses and the manner in which he places items

within them tend to reflect his *pro* or *con* attitude. As we have noted in various contexts, the result is frequently considerable displacement of items, particularly those items which are ambiguous or ambivalent.

It is rather well known that when an individual is told that his attitudes are the subject of investigation, he can "correct" for his personal bias and respond as he thinks the experimenter or his contemporaries expect him to. In the Hammond study cited in the last chapter (p. 96), the single notation "Att-Info" on a test form was sufficient to produce differential choices by the subjects, as compared with the notation "Info" alone.

In the experiments reported above, the subjects were not instructed to place items in terms of their attitudes on the issue, but in terms of social realities. Despite this fact, their attitudes were revealed in the placement of items (particularly the neutral or ambiguous items), in the number of categories used, and in the frequency of their use. This finding supports the possibility of motivation-attitude research using techniques which do not appear to the subjects as a test of their attitudes. If future investigations bear out the promise of our results, it may prove feasible to order the stands of individuals on a controversial social issue through their placements of relevant items within their "own" categories. As an "indirect" or "disguised" technique for attitude measurement, this procedure would have great advantage for experimentation in the motivation-attitude area over conventional techniques which directly question the subject's agreement and disagreement with various items. When direct questions are used, the subject is put on guard. Results may be artifacts which are not valid data for the problem under investigation. The investigation of attitudes will proceed more rapidly and profitably when a behavioral index of the individual's attitude, based on performance in a task apparently unrelated to his attitudes, can be utilized in research practice.

CHAPTER 6

Latitudes of Acceptance and Rejection on Social Issues

IN THE PRECEDING CHAPTERS, the placement of stimulus items into categories was analyzed in terms of reciprocal relationships between the individual's scale and those factors functioning as anchorages. In the last two chapters we have seen that internal factors, as well as aspects of the external stimulus situation, may function as anchors in the placement of an item. The individual's own stand on a social issue, for example, can serve as the main anchor in his judgment of statements related to it. One's position in social arrangements or his status relative to the known achievements of others becomes an anchor for making estimates of his own performance.

In social judgments more than one anchor is usually involved. In Marks' study of judgments of skin color, reported in Chapter 4 (p. 91), the following four determinants were apparent: the skin color of the rater, the generally preferred skin color in the group, the objective skin color of the person rated, and the feeling toward the person rated. The simultaneous functioning of several anchors in judgment is not peculiar to social judgment, however. There have been experiments using weights or other simple stimuli in which a standard stimulus and another interpolated anchor have each had a demonstrable effect on judgments of a stimulus series (Woodworth and Schlosberg, 1954, p. 228f.).

On the basis of studies of social judgment, we can predict that an established attitude provides an anchor in appraising a communication pertinent to it. Communication, particularly persuasive communication, may be conceived as another anchor in the judgment situation. Thus, the initial step in study of the individual's reaction to a communication is to examine the relationship between an advocated position and the individual's stand prior to exposure. The experiments summarized in this and the next chapter are attempts toward more systematic study of this relationship.

Let us consider these two anchors which are involved when the individual is exposed to a communication on a social issue toward which he has taken a stand. The communication advocates a position which can be located relative to a series of other positions on the issue. The individual's placement and appraisal of the communication are affected by its position relative to prevailing social realities and in addition by the effectiveness of presentation, the source of the communication, and the individual's relation to the source. The individual's stand prior to exposure to communication may also be represented as a position relative to the same series of stands on the issue. Most of the conventional tests or scales for attitude measurement yield a score or index which purports to locate the individual's stand on an issue relative to other stands currently prevailing in a society. However, we cannot assume that a single position in the series adequately represents the individual's stand for the purpose of understanding his reactions to relevant stimuli, such as a communication. His stand on the issue may incorporate several adjacent positions which he accepts or tolerates (cf. Sherif and Sherif, 1956, pp. 532–3; Sherif, 1960).

In this chapter, the individual's stand on a social issue is conceived as a range or a *latitude of acceptance*. A latitude of acceptance for certain stands on an issue implies a rather definite range of rejection as well. It is defined operationally as the range of the positions on an issue that an individual considers acceptable to him (including the one "most acceptable" to him). The *latitude of rejection* consists of the positions he finds objectionable (including the one "most objectionable" to him).

A brief illustration can indicate the rationale for investigating the latitudes of acceptance and rejection. Let us represent a series of positions on a social issue by the letters A through I. Now let two persons each choose position B in this series as the position most acceptable to him. Suppose, however, that one finds only position A tolerable in addition to B, and rejects all positions from C through I. The second finds all positions acceptable until he comes to position E. It seems entirely reasonable that a communication presenting, say the E position, would be reacted to differently by these two individuals. The first individual would probably find the communication considerably more objectionable than the latter.

As their names imply, the latitudes of acceptance and rejection are conceived in motivational terms. The degree of the individual's personal involvement in an issue should be closely related to important characteristics of his latitudes of acceptance and rejection. In the last chapter we summarized a study in which strongly ego-involved subjects were instructed to use eleven categories for judgment of favorableness-unfavorableness. Despite the instructions, they neglected certain categories, and the distribution of their judgments was closely related to their agreement or disagreement with the positions which the categories represented. These highly ego-involved subjects placed a large number of the items in the extreme categories with which they strongly disagreed and relatively fewer in the extreme categories with which they agreed. When given the opportunity to sort the same items into the number of categories they thought necessary, the highly involved subjects used fewer categories than less involved subjects and continued to pile up items at the end of the scale they rejected. From these results we infer that the highly ego-involved subjects had a more constricted latitude of acceptance and a more extensive latitude of rejection than the less involved subjects.

Thus it would seem that high ego-involvement with an issue produces a raised threshold for acceptance of positions on the issue, a relationship which results in an extensive latitude of rejection. The person who zealously upholds a position tends to be quite particular about accepting other positions and is likely to see the rest of the world as opposed to his stand— "those who are not for us are against us."

A finding by Cartwright (1941) concerning political attitudes is pertinent. "For the radical S, the judgments of 'radical' extend 7.5 units while the judgments of 'conservative' extend 10 units. For the conservative S, on the other hand, the judgments of 'radical' extend 8.5 units, while the judgments of 'conservative' extend only 5.2 units," (p. 189). In addition, he reported: "The size of the range of equivalence related to a 'radical' and to a 'conservative' differed, depending upon S's own political attitudes" (p. 195). In a study of attitudes toward war and censorship among college students, Johnson (1955) noted that subjects holding extreme positions gave many more negative judgments with greater confidence than those with moderate positions on the issues.

LATITUDES OF ACCEPTANCE AND REJECTION ON CONTROVERSIAL ISSUES

In order to investigate some relationships between the individual's own stand on an issue and the position of a communication, we studied the latitudes of acceptance and rejection for individuals holding different positions on controversial social issues. The results of these studies and their implications constitute the remainder of this chapter.

As a first step in comparative research, controversial social issues were chosen in which known groups of individuals are considerably ego-involved. The first of these was prohibition, an issue hardly affecting most citizens, but a lively topic among residents of the remaining "dry" areas. The study on the prohibition issue (Hovland, Harvey, and Sherif, 1957) was carried out in the dry state of Oklahoma shortly after a referendum was held to determine the fate of its prohibition laws. The vote favored prohibition by a narrow margin. The second study utilized the issue of the 1956 national presidential campaign during the weeks preceding the election. In both studies, steps were taken to insure that highly ego-involved individuals would be included by selecting some subjects from groups with known public commitments and a record of active support of a partisan stand.

Several existing attitude tests are useful in ranking individuals relative to the extreme positions on an issue. In order to determine their latitudes of acceptance and rejection, however, it was necessary to devise techniques to determine the number and location of items with which the individual agreed, disagreed, or on which he was noncommittal.

Studies of the Prohibition Issue and the 1956 Presidential Campaign

The general procedures were similar in our experiments on the prohibition issue and the 1956 presidential election. Following an account of procedures and the statements prepared in each study to secure latitudes of acceptance and rejection, the results will be summarized.

The experiments were carried out in two sessions. The first session was devoted entirely to securing data on the position on the issue which was most acceptable to the subject and the range of his tolerance for other positions (his latitude of acceptance); the position most objectionable to him and the range of stands he rejected (latitude of rejection); and finally those stands which he considered neither acceptable nor unacceptable.

During the second session, each group of subjects heard a tape recording which was introduced as a talk by a proponent of the stand advocated. The source was not otherwise specified. In each experiment, three communications were used, each presenting a different stand. The communication which a particular group of subjects heard was selected so that varying discrepancies between the position of communication and the subjects' initial position were represented. Following the communication, the schedules for securing latitudes of acceptance and rejection were filled in a second time and reactions to the communication were obtained. Findings in the second session are presented in the next chapter. In the present context, we are interested in the subjects' judgments in the first session.

Determining latitudes of acceptance and rejection. In order to secure differentiated stands from prevailing opinion on the prohibition issue, representative statements made during the referendum campaign were collected from leading newspapers in two large cities and statements of opinion were obtained from five hundred people in several localities. Twenty judges sorted these statements and eight statements were chosen as representing clearly differentiated positions actually taken in the state. These statements ranged from strong advocacy of prohibition to strong advocacy of repeal. An additional "wet" statement was added as a logical counterpart of the most extreme "dry" stand, giving a total of nine statements. It should be noted that no assumptions (e.g. that intervals between the positions were equidistant) were made about these statements other than that prevailing stands on the issue were represented and arranged in rank order.

The nine final statements are as follows, statement (I) being the additional item:

(A) Since alcohol is the curse of mankind, the sale and use of alcohol, including light beer, should be completely abolished.

(B) Since alcohol is the main cause of corruption in public life, lawlessness, and immoral acts, its sale and use should be prohibited.

(C) Since it is hard to stop at a reasonable moderation point in the use of alcohol, it is safer to discourage its use.

(D) Alcohol should not be sold or used except as a remedy for snake bites, cramps, colds, fainting, and other aches and pains.

(E) The arguments in favor and against the sale and use of alchohol are nearly equal.

(F) The sale of alcohol should be so regulated that it is available in limited quantities for special occasions.

(G) The sale and use of alcohol should be permitted with proper state controls, so that the revenue from taxation may be used for the betterment of schools, highways, and other state institutions.

(H) Since prohibition is a major cause of corruption in public life, lawlessness, immoral acts, and juvenile delinquency, the sale and use of alcohol should be legalized.

(I) It has become evident that man cannot get along without alcohol; therefore there should be no restriction whatsoever on its sale and use.

The subjects were instructed to read the statements carefully, and then, successively, to indicate the one statement coming closest to their own stands on the issue, other statements not objectionable to them, the most objectionable statement, and other statements objectionable to them.

These procedures gave the subject an opportunity to take a stand or not to take a stand on any item and avoided artificial indifference or neutral checkings. Thus they approximate actual situations confronting individuals with stimulus items on which they are not ready to take definite stands.

Since the prohibition issue was chosen to secure ego-involved subjects, a special point was made of obtaining subjects with established and publicly committed dry or wet stands on the issue. Individuals from Women's Christian Temperance Union groups and Salvation Army workers were used, as well as students preparing for the ministry or attending strict denominational colleges in Oklahoma. A total of 183 dry subjects participated in this study. Organized groups with a wet stand were difficult to find in Oklahoma at the time. Twenty-five wet subjects were selected from small informal groups known personally to the experimenters. For comparison, 290 additional subjects represented more moderate stands on the issue. These were college students at a state university where sentiment, on the whole, favored a moderately wet stand. Because of the importance of securing highly ego-involved subjects, it was not possible to match the age levels of subjects in the three categories.

Latitudes of acceptance and rejection on the prohibition issue. The data show the stand a subject chose to represent his own position, the other stands which were not objectionable, the stand most clearly opposed to his position, others not acceptable, and those stands on which he was noncommittal. Thus the relative position of a subject's stand as well as its extent and the area of rejection can be specified.

First let us compare the number of items on the prohibition issue rated acceptable, objectionable, and neither acceptable nor objectionable by individuals with (1) extreme positions (A, B, or G, H, I) and with (2) intermediate positions (C, D, E, F). Table 1 presents this comparison in terms of the mean number of items checked. From this comparison we find that individuals with extreme positions tend to reject more frequently positions not within their latitudes of acceptance; subjects with intermediate stands are more apt to rate positions removed from their own as indifferent. It will be observed that significantly more items are judged unaccept-

TABLE 1. *Mean number of statements acceptable, neither acceptable nor unacceptable, and objectionable to subjects with extreme positions and intermediate positions. (From Hovland, Harvey, and Sherif, 1957.)*

Subjects' positions	N	Mean number of items acceptable	Mean number of items not checked	Mean number of items rejected
Extreme (A,B,G,H,I)	193	2.81	1.48	4.71
Intermediate (C,D,E,F)	37	3.05	2.24	3.70
p				<.03

able by subjects with extreme stands. Smaller differences between the groups are obtained in the number rated acceptable.

These data suggest that subjects with extreme positions on an issue use wider categories for rejection than for acceptance and employ a wider category for rejection than those with intermediate positions.

Relative size of latitudes of acceptance and rejection on the election issue. The latitudes of acceptance and rejection exhibited by individuals holding extreme stands and moderate stands suggested the following hypothesis:

The latitude of rejection of individuals upholding an extreme stand on an ego-involving issue is greater than the latitude of rejection of individuals holding a moderate position on the same issue.

As a corollary to this hypothesis, it was expected that the latitudes of rejection of individuals upholding an extreme stand on an ego-involving issue will be relatively greater than their latitudes of acceptance.

Data pertinent to the hypothesis and its corollary were obtained in the election study. The election issue was suitable for investigating these propositions because adequate numbers of subjects with differing stands were available.

Nine statements were chosen on the basis of trials with twenty-five individuals whose stands were known to the experimenters and whose preferences ranged from extreme partisanship for the election of Republican presidential and vice-presidential candidates to extreme partisanship for Democratic candidates. The nine statements, ranging from extreme partisanship for the Republican candidates (designated A position) through the middle-of-the-road position (E position) to extreme partisanship for the Democratic candidates (I position) were as follows:

(A) The election of the Republican presidential and vice-presidential candidates in November is absolutely essential from all angles in the country's interests.

(B) On the whole the interests of the country will be served best by the election of the Republican candidates for president and vice-president in the coming election.

(C) It seems that the country's interests would be better served if the presidential and vice-presidential candidates of the Republican party are elected this November.

(D) Although it is hard to decide, it is probable that the country's interests may be better served if the Republican presidential candidates are elected in November.

(E) From the point of view of the country's interests, it is hard to decide whether it is preferable to vote for presidential and vice-presidential candidates of the Republican party or the Democratic party in November.

(F) Although it is hard to decide, it is probable that the country's interests may be better served if the Democratic presidential and vice-presidential candidates are elected in November.

(G) It seems that the country's interests would be better served if the presidential and vice-presidential candidates of the Democratic party are elected this November.

(H) On the whole the interests of the country will be served best if the presidential and vice-presidential candidates of the Democratic party are elected this November.

(I) The election of the Democratic presidential and vice-presidential candidates in November is absolutely essential from all angles in the country's interests.

The complete set of statements from A to I was mimeographed on each of four sheets of paper. On the first sheet, subjects indicated the "most acceptable" statement, on the second other statements "not objectionable," on the third sheet the "most objectionable" statement, and on the last sheet "other objectionable" statements.

The results pertaining to latitudes of acceptance and rejection are based on data from 406 subjects who participated in the first session of this study. The subjects were college population (undergraduate and graduate) in three universities in the southwest. The sessions were conducted on the college premises either in classroom units or specially arranged groups (Young Republicans, League of Young Democrats, or small dormitory units). The median age for the total sample was slightly above 21 years.

We shall consider A, B, and C as extreme positions favoring the election of Republican candidates; G, H, and I as extreme positions favoring the Democratic candidates; and D,

E, and F as moderate positions between the two extremes. Symmetry was not the main purpose of the threefold division of the positions represented. Schisms in social life are seldom this symmetrical.

Our classification is based on empirical grounds. The end positions (A and I) were worded very strongly by intent. Among the subjects were members of political organizations active in the campaign. Some of these persons were disrupting the routine of their daily lives to contribute to the victory of their candidates. However, most of these subjects checked either B or H position as most acceptable, and they were not unanimous in endorsing the A or I positions. In fact, only about 46 per cent of the subjects checking B or H position as most acceptable selected A or I position as also acceptable to them. Nearly 20 per cent of the subjects at B or H position rejected the statements at the nearby extreme. On the other hand, no less than 90 per cent of subjects checking B or H positions as most acceptable included, respectively, the C or G statements in their latitudes of acceptance. Therefore, the C and G positions were included within the two extreme segments in our analysis.

The latitudes of acceptance ($\vee\vee + \vee$) and rejection (XX + X) and the number not checked (o) were determined for each individual. The frequencies of $\vee\vee + \vee$, XX + X, and o (noncommittal) responses were computed for each position on the issue. The proportions of items accepted, rejected, and not checked by subjects holding each of the nine positions are presented in Table 2.

In Table 2, it can be seen that the proportion of items included in the latitude of acceptance is smaller than that for the latitude of rejection under each position except at F where it is slightly greater. However, the differences for extreme positions A, B, C and G, H, I are greater in every case than the differences for moderate positions (D, E, and F).

Inspection of Table 2 reveals that individuals holding extreme positions reject a considerably greater proportion of items than they accept. Thus the findings support our expectation that individuals holding an extreme stand would reject relatively more positions than they would accept. Yet the proportion of items acceptable to individuals at the

TABLE 2. *Per cent of positions on the election issue included in the latitude of acceptance ($\sqrt{\sqrt{}} + \sqrt{} =$ strongly accept plus accept), latitude of rejection (XX + X = strongly reject plus reject), and noncommittal reactions (0 = neither accept nor reject) by subjects checking each position as most acceptable.*

Positions checked most acceptable	$(\sqrt{\sqrt{}} + \sqrt{})$	(XX + X)	(0)	$(\sqrt{\sqrt{}} + \sqrt{}) - (XX + X)$
A	37.02	51.38	11.60	−14.36
B	33.37	52.29	14.34	−18.92
C	35.19	48.56	16.25	−13.37
D	33.33	40.33	26.33	−7.00
E	32.24	38.43	29.32	−6.19
F	40.66	39.56	19.78	1.10
G	36.46	43.65	19.89	−7.19
H	35.21	53.72	11.07	−18.51
I	30.56	55.56	13.88	−25.00

various positions does not differ appreciably. The differences lie in the greater frequency of rejections by individuals at the extreme positions and relatively more noncommittal reactions by individuals in the middle. Percentages for latitudes of rejection decrease as one moves from extreme to middle positions along with marked increases in noncommittal reactions.

In confirmation of these trends, the great majority of individuals with extreme stands had latitudes of acceptance smaller than their own latitudes of rejection, while more than half of the moderate subjects had latitudes of acceptance equal to or greater than their latitudes of rejection. A chi-square test of these frequencies showed the differences are significant.

We may conclude that the relative sizes of the latitudes of acceptance and rejection on an ego-involving issue differ significantly for groups holding extreme positions as compared with groups holding moderate positions on the issue. The latitude of rejection is greater for subjects with extreme stands and smaller for subjects holding moderate positions. These differences cannot be explained as an artifact caused by concentration of acceptances at the ends and lack of available positions beyond the extreme ends of the scale. In fact, our results reveal a reluctance to endorse the extreme end items, even by subjects selecting a position next to the end as the one "most acceptable." These results are in line with the trends obtained in the prohibition study reported earlier (pp. 132–135).

More recently, La Fave and Sherif (1959) tested the hypothesis using a different issue and different procedures. In order to insure that individuals varying in ego-involvement in the issue were included, they chose subjects from a Negro university in a large southwestern city, from several chapters of a Southern white fraternity which had the reputation of being prosegregationist, and from classes in an integrated university. With no mention of their own attitudes on the issue being made, the subjects were instructed to categorize a series of brief descriptions of behavior according to the position these behaviors represented on the segregation-desegration issue. They were free to use any number of categories they chose to represent different positions on the issue. After making their judgments, the subjects were asked to indicate the category containing items most acceptable to them, any other category or categories which might also be acceptable, and the most objectionable category of items plus other objectionable categories.

The relative sizes of the latitudes of acceptance and rejection were determined by counting the number of items placed in those categories labeled acceptable and objectionable, respectively. More frequently than committed subjects, unselected subjects had latitudes of acceptance equal to or larger than their latitudes of rejection, while Negro subjects and anti-Negro white subjects more frequently placed fewer items in categories which they labeled as acceptable than in categories labeled objectionable. The trend was stronger for Negro subjects than for the white members of the Southern fraternity; however the latter groups included some subjects who by their own self-ratings after the judgment task were not anti-integration. In view of the doubtful character of self-ratings on this issue in university settings largely favorable to integration, the objective criterion, viz. membership in the fraternity group, was used in the analysis. There was also a trend for a larger proportion of unselected subjects to leave one or more categories unlabeled (as neither acceptable nor objectionable) than of subjects with extreme stands. Therefore, these findings support the hypothesis investigated in the studies of the prohibition and election issues using a different issue and different procedures.

AN EMPIRICAL MODEL OF LATITUDES OF ACCEPTANCE AND REJECTION

Knowledge of the patterning of latitudes of acceptance and rejection for individuals upholding different stands on a controversial issue should be useful in investigating reactions to communication. For example, if the position advo-

cated in a communication falls within an individual's latitude of rejection, a favorable evaluation of the communication would hardly be expected.

The procedures for determining the latitudes of acceptance and rejection used in the prohibition and election
studies yield data suitable for constructing a model. In the
prohibition study, data on certain positions were sparse. As a
first approximation, we proceeded on the basis of the results
on the relative size of latitudes of acceptance and rejection
for subjects with extreme and moderate stands (Table 2) and
of deductions from our previous studies on placement of
items on the Negro issue. A hypothetical pattern was constructed of the expected latitudes of acceptance and rejection for individuals upholding each initial position on the
prohibition issue. Where sufficient numbers of subjects endorsing a given stand were available in the prohibition study,
the hypothetical pattern is in close correspondence with empirical distributions of responses to the various items. The
formal pattern is presented in Table 3.

In Table 3, the individual's own position on the issue is
indicated in the columns, and the items rated (statements
A–I) are indicated in the rows. The subject's own stand is
indicated by $\sqrt{\sqrt{}}$, also acceptable with $\sqrt{}$, completely unacceptable with XX, other stands unacceptable with X, and
neither acceptable or unacceptable with o. Thus the items
marked $\sqrt{\sqrt{}}$ and $\sqrt{}$ represent the latitude of acceptance, and
those marked XX and X the latitude of rejection for Ss
holding each position. It was expected that the relative sizes
of the latitudes of acceptance and rejection would vary as a
function of the degree of ego-involvement. A person strongly
committed on the issue would be more discriminating in accepting stands (raised threshold of acceptance) and less discriminating in rejecting stands (lowered threshold of rejection). Thus, in the table, the latitudes of acceptance for more

ego-involved subjects are represented as smaller than their latitudes of rejection, the latter increasing in extent as the subject's own position becomes more extreme.

In the election study, sufficient numbers of subjects were available to compare the locations of latitudes of acceptance and rejection for subjects at different positions. Table 4 sum-

TABLE 3. *Hypothetical latitudes of acceptance and rejection of subjects holding each position*

Subject's own position

Positions rated	A	B	C	D	E	F	G	H	I
A	√√	√	0	X	X	XX	XX	XX	XX
B	√	√√	√	0	X	X	X	X	X
C	0	√	√√	√	0	X	X	X	X
D	X	0	√	√√	√	0	X	X	X
E	X	X	0	√	√√	√	0	X	X
F	X	X	X	0	√	√√	√	0	X
G	X	X	X	X	0	√	√√	√	0
H	X	X	X	X	X	0	√	√√	√
I	XX	XX	XX	XX	X	X	0	√	√√

Mean item frequencies in above table

	A,B,C	D,E,F	G,H,I
√√ and √	2.7	3.0	2.7
0	1.3	2.0	1.3
X and XX	5.0	4.0	5.0

marizes the locations of latitude of acceptance and rejection, using 50 per cent of responses in a given classification as the cutting point. The items marked √√ and √ represent the latitude of acceptance for subjects upholding a given "own position" based on items endorsed by 50 per cent or more of the subjects in that classification. Obtained percentages are given below the response category in each cell. The items marked XX and X represent the latitude of rejection based on the same criterion. Positions toward which 50 per cent or more of the subjects with a given "own position" remained noncommittal are indicated by the symbol o.

For some positions, no response category reached the 50

TABLE 4. *Percentages showing obtained latitudes of acceptance and rejection for subjects holding each position on the election issue*

Subject's own position

Positions rated	A	B	C	D	E	F	G	H	I
A	√√	√	0	X	XX	XX	XX	XX	XX
	100	*45.8*	*45.6*	65.2	82.4	96.7	100	100	100
B	√	√√	√	0	X	X	X	X	X
	100	100	85.3	*47.8*	50	80	85	100	100
C	√	√	√√	√	0	X	X	X	X
	100	98.3	100	73.9	*41.2*	66.7	70	98.4	100
D	0	√	√	√√	√	0	X	X	X
	50	*43.7*	69.9	100	66.2	*43.3*	60	88.5	87.5
E	X	X	0	√	√√	√	0	X	X
	65	55.1	*45.6*	60.9	100	66.7	*45*	*47.6*	75
F	X	X	X	X	√	√√	·√	√	0
	77.5	77.3	69.1	*43.5*	53	100	70	50	50
G	X	X	X	X	0	√	√√	√	√
	90	97.5	86.8	58.7	56	90	100	91.8	50
H	X	X	X	X	0	√	√	√√	√
	100	98.3	92.7	58.7	53	60	85	100	100
I	XX	XX	XX	XX	XX	X	X	√	√√
	100	99.2	98.5	97.8	82.4	63.3	*40*	*46.7*	100

* Percentages italicized refer to the response given with greatest frequency to items where no response reached the criterion of 50%.

Mean item frequencies in above table using 50 per cent criterion

	A,B,C	D,E,F	G,H,I
√√ + √	2.66	3.33	3.00
0	.33	.66	.33
XX + X	4.66	3.66	4.33
Items not meeting 50% criterion	1.33	1.33	1.33

per cent cutting point. In these instances, the category used by the greatest proportion of the subjects with a given own position is presented along with its symbol. These symbols and percentages are italicized to indicate that the criterion was not met. The italicized cells indicate, therefore, regions where responses of a given subject group were mixed.

This table may be compared to Table 3 presenting hypothetical latitudes of acceptance and rejection for the prohibition issue. Despite the fact that Table 3 pertains to an entirely different issue (prohibition), and an adequate number of subjects, especially on the extreme wet side, were not available to base it entirely on empirical findings, the over-all pattern is remarkably similar to that in Table 4, presenting obtained data for the election issue.

The resemblance of the formalized pattern for the prohibition issue and the pattern based on obtained data for the election issue using a 50 per cent cutting point is sufficiently close to warrant further investigation. Thorough investigation of the patterns of latitudes of acceptance and rejection and the regions of noncommitment may permit much more efficient design of experiments varying the position of a communication on an issue relative to an individual's stand and result in increased precision in prediction of his reactions to it.

CHAPTER 7

Reactions to Communication and Attitude Change

IN THE PRESENT CHAPTER the concepts and empirical relationships derived from studies of judgment are applied to an analysis of the effects of communication.

The literature on the effects of communication on attitudes has been reviewed by a number of authors (Hovland, 1954; Murphy, Murphy, and Newcomb, 1937; Sherif and Sherif, 1956). One of the puzzles in this literature is the lack of consistency in the findings. Thus in their survey, Murphy, Murphy, and Newcomb observed that studies of attitude change through communication had yielded three characteristic distributions of attitude scores. A few studies reported no substantial change following communication. A more frequent finding was shift in the distribution toward the position taken in the communication. A third and not infrequent finding following communication was a bimodal distribution, revealing shifts *toward* communication by some subjects and *away* from communication by other subjects.

For example, Remmers (1938) obtained positive shifts in average test scores following communications on conservation, social insurance, and labor unions, but the latter communication "sharply divided the group into two opposing tents" (p. 201).

In Knower's study (1935) prior to repeal of prohibition,

"wet" communications to generally "dry" subjects and "dry" communications to generally "wet" subjects resulted in shifts in both positive and negative directions in each group. A rather striking instance of such opposing effects was reported by Wilke (1934), whose antiwar communication was presented at a time when the student population from which the subjects were drawn was divided in controversy over that very issue.

A few studies, such as those by Manske (1937) and Russell and Robertson (1947), have found group shifts in the direction opposite to the stand presented in communication. A related finding, reported by Williams and Remmers (1939) following communication on a rural issue, was reduced variability and a less favorable stand by a group of rural youth in comparison with the increased variability in an urban group. Some authors who have obtained results in the direction away from communication suggested that too great divergence between the subject's stand on the issue and the stand presented in communication may have been responsible.

The implication of our previous chapters is that the effect of a communication will depend to a major extent on its relationship to the position of the recipient and his latitudes of acceptance and rejection. On the whole, the relationship between the positions of a communication and the recipient has been a neglected topic of research, possibly because the emphasis in earlier studies was on how much change would occur under varying conditions. Perhaps the focus should be shifted from the end product (that is, attitude change) to underlying processes and intervening events (cf. Hovland, 1951; Sherif and Sherif, 1956, pp. 762–75). Then more satisfactory explanations may be formulated of why change, no change, and change in a direction opposed to communication can occur in response to the same communication.

PLACEMENT OF COMMUNICATION

One implication of the preceding chapters concerns the way an individual will interpret the material presented to him (in this case, a complex communication). If the results cited in Chapter 5 on displacement of attitude items are applicable to entire communications, as we would expect them to be, the perceived position of a communication should be different for individuals with varying initial stands on the issue. The effect should be particularly marked when a communication attempts to advocate a position in the middle range, because positions in the moderate and neutral area are more susceptible to alternative interpretations.

The two studies discussed in the preceding chapter were also designed to investigate the effect of the recipient's own position on his placement of the position of the communication. The first communication concerned the prohibition issue in a dry state where repeal of prohibition statutes had recently been defeated, and the other the presidential campaign in the weeks just preceding the 1956 election. The general procedures, selection of subjects, and results on the latitudes of acceptance and rejection in these two experiments have already been described.

The design of the experiments permitted an analysis of the placement of the position advocated in the communication by the subjects, their favorable or unfavorable reactions to the communication, and the direction and amount of change by subjects whose attitudes differed in varying degrees from the position advocated in communication. In each experiment, three communications advocating different positions were presented. In order that the subject's stand on the issue be the main internal anchor, the source of the communication was not specified beyond stating that the speech had been made by an advocate of the position.

The hypotheses tested concern the relationship between the subject's position and that advocated in the communication. To the extent that the communication was ambiguous, displacements could be expected in the judgment of the position it advocated. If the individual's stand on the issue were the main anchor and his stand differed greatly from that presented, it was predicted that the position of the communication would be displaced *away* from his own stand. More formally stated the first hypothesis was as follows:

When the position in communication is susceptible to alternative interpretations, displacements of the position advocated will vary as a function of its distance from the subject's stand. The greater the discrepancy between the subject's own stand and the position advocated, the greater the displacement away from the subject's position ("contrast effect"). When only a small discrepancy in positions exists, there will be a tendency for displacement toward his own stand ("assimilation effect").

We would not expect that a communication taking a clearly black or white stand on an issue would be subject to much displacement by individuals exposed to it. The clever communicator advocating an extreme stand ordinarily seeks to influence through disguising his stand, precisely because its position is easily located by most individuals when it is not disguised. However, communications presenting more moderate stands might be expected to undergo some displacement because the relative positions between the extreme regions are simply more difficult to ascertain (cf. Chapters 3 and 5).

Therefore we asked subjects who listened to a moderately

wet communication to indicate on a graphic scale ranging from the extreme dry position to the extreme wet position, what they thought the position of the communication to be. (The communication represented the F position in the statements on prohibition presented in the last chapter.)

In Figure 15 results are presented. The subject's own position is indicated on the abscissa and along the ordinate the

Figure 15. Average Placement of Position of Moderately Wet Communication by Subjects Holding Various Positions on the Issue, with Superimposed Hypothetical Assimilation-Contrast Curve

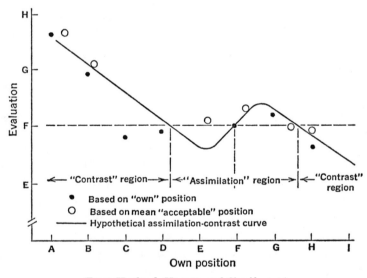

(From Hovland, Harvey, and Sherif 1957.)

average rating of the position of the communication. The dots indicate the mean placement of the position of the communication for subjects who checked each particular position as their own stand. The circles represent the mean placement of the position advocated when the subject's position is estimated from the mean of his latitude of acceptance. The dotted line indicates a hypothetical relationship in which individuals holding the same position as the communication report its position accurately (at F), those a small distance removed assimilate it to their own position, and those still further removed exaggerate the distance between their own stand and the communication, revealing a contrast effect.

The expectation is fulfilled that those upholding wet stands judge that the communication advocated a drier position than it did, and those with extremely dry stands judge that it was advocating a wetter position than it did. Those nearer the position of the communication reported it more objectively. The evidence concerning assimilation deviates somewhat from the theoretical curve. There were too few subjects with intermediate positions to enable us to determine these positions adequately.

Comparable data were obtained on placement of communications on the 1956 presidential campaign. The greatest displacement was predicted for judgment of the communication presenting a middle position (position E in the nine statements on the election), which briefly stated the claims of the two major parties on various campaign issues without taking sides or drawing clear conclusions. Although displacements are not large, pro-Republican subjects tended to place the E communication toward the pro-Democratic segment with a median rating of 5.2, and pro-Democratic subjects displaced the communication toward pro-Republican positions with a median rating of 4.68. Subjects with moderate and middle positions placed the communication more accurately (median rating of 5.00).

Because the distributions of the ratings by subjects with extreme views tended toward bimodality, a further analysis was made of these data in terms of frequency of accurate placement and of displacement toward or away from one's own position by subjects upholding different stands. With placement at E represented by 5, placement between 4.5 and 5.5 was made by about one-fourth of the subjects. Of the subjects checking moderate or the middle positions as their own stand (D, F, or E), equal numbers displaced the E communication toward the Democratic segment (5.5 or above) and toward the Republican segment (4.5 or below). In comparison, significantly larger proportions of pro-Republican (A, B, C positions) and pro-Democratic subjects (G, H, I) displaced the communication *away* from their own positions.

However, the small proportion of subjects exposed to the middle communication on the 1956 election issue who displaced its position toward their own stand (assimilation), instead of away from it requires further comment. This trend is not in line with our hypothesis. A communication at *dead center,* which takes no position on the issue, may be subject to both contrast and assimilation effects, and our formulation has to be expanded to handle communications of this nature. The middle communication on the election issue presented both sides and did not draw conclusions. As a result conclusions could be drawn in either direction. To investigate this possibility, research was undertaken by Sherif immediately prior to the 1960 presidential election in Oklahoma and the Pacific Northwest. In addition to a middle communication drawing no conclusions, two moderate communications were presented, one moderately pro-Republican and one moderately pro-Democratic. The use of these additional communications may clarify reactions to the middle communication.

The strongly pro-Republican communication and the strongly pro-Democratic communication were accurately placed at positions A and I, respectively, by the overwhelming majority of subjects who heard them. Average errors of placement were very small for both communications. There were tendencies, though not large, for subjects at middle positions to perceive the communications as less extreme than did subjects upholding strongly pro-Democratic or pro-Republican stands. Of greater importance, however, is the clear finding that undisguised extreme communications were not subject to appreciable displacements by any subject groups, regardless of their own stands on the issue.

Recent research by Manis (1960 a, b, c) is pertinent to our findings. The communications used by Manis were statements written by college undergraduates concerning their views (pro, neutral, anti) on college fraternities. The subject's task was to predict how the writer of each communication would respond on six evaluative scales (e.g. good-bad) in rating the concept "college fraternities." Manis reports a curvilinear relationship between mean predictions and the subjects' attitudes for the pro and antifraternity communications. A comparison of the results in his two studies conducted on different university campuses (1960 a, 1960 b) suggests that the curvilinearity is largely attributable to the tendency of neutral subjects to assimilate the pro and anti communications to their own more moderate positions, in line with the trend in the 1956 election study. For the neutral communication, however, a linear relationship between attitude and placement of the communication was found in both experiments, i.e. individuals who opposed fraternities made more antifraternity predictions than those who favored fraternities. This is an *assimilation* trend.

In Chapter 3 the effects of varying sources of communication were discussed briefly, with particular reference to the possibility that a prestigeful source would extend the assimilation range. Manis (1960 c) varied the source by attributing some messages to outstanding, stable, mature, well-

bred, and respected students and others to students with opposite traits. Predictions of the position of high prestige
sources were linearly related to the subjects' attitudes on
the issue for all three communications (anti, neutral, pro).
In short, the assimilation effect was general. The only consistent effect produced by attributing the messages to a low-
prestige student was to shift all predictions by profraternity
and neutral subjects toward antifraternity ratings. Perhaps
the descriptions of the low-prestige source (as being asked
to leave school, as unstable and neurotic, unpopular and
unreliable) fit the stereotypes these students had regarding
those taking an antifraternity position.

EVALUATION OF COMMUNICATION AS A FUNCTION OF OWN POSITION

The results in Chapter 6 on the latitudes of acceptance and
rejection suggest that there will be marked differences in the
evaluations of an identical communication as a function of
the recipient's stand on the issue. The findings of the two
communication experiments were analyzed to determine
how the position of the recipient would influence his evaluation. A five-item scale was used to measure evaluation of the
fairness and impartiality of the communication. In Figure
16 the percentages of subjects in each group whose reactions
were favorable are represented for the three communications
on the prohibition issue. On the abscissa, the stands of the
recipient (mean of his latitude of acceptance) are presented
and on the ordinate the percentage of favorable evaluations.

There is an extremely close relationship between the individual's own stand on the issue and his evaluation of communication. The two communications advocating extreme
positions have their peak of favorable response among those
holding corresponding extreme positions. The maximum
favorable reaction for the moderate communication is found

among those holding a moderate position. The data provide quantitative information to support the expectation from earlier studies (Hovland, Janis, and Kelley, 1953) that individuals who are in favor of the opinion advocated will consider the communication fair and unbiased, but that those with an opposed stand will regard the identical communication as propagandistic and unfair.

Figure 16. Percentage of Favorable Evaluations of Wet, Moderately Wet, and Dry Communications by Subjects Holding Various Positions on Prohibition

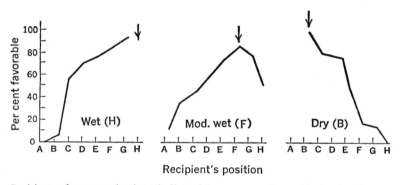

Positions of communications indicated by arrows. (From Hovland, Harvey, and Sherif 1957.)

Essentially similar results were obtained on evaluations of the pro-Republican and pro-Democratic communications by recipients with different stands on the 1956 election. The percentages of favorable evaluations of the three communications in that study are shown in Table 5. The two communications presenting extreme stands were evaluated most favorably by partisans of the party advocated and with very little favorable reaction among the opponents of that stand. The subject's position in this table is based on the mean position he checked as acceptable.

TABLE 5. *Percentage of favorable evaluations of communications for subjects with different stands on election*

Subject stand (mean latitude of acceptance)	Position of communication		
	REPUBLICAN	DEMOCRATIC	MIDDLE
A			
	100.0	0.0	77.2
B			
	90.5	10.2	60.0
C			
	75.0	7.0	70.0
D			
	25.0	17.8	55.5
E			
	30.0	50.0	50.0
F			
	11.7	64.3	68.7
G			
	2.2	83.3	37.5
H			
	0.0	—	0.0
I			

Evaluations of the middle communication, which presented both sides without drawing definite conclusions, differ somewhat from those for the moderately wet communication (at F) on the prohibition issue. The peak for favorable reactions is among subjects with strongly pro-Republican stands (positions A–C) rather than the middle position. The results for pro-Democratic subjects are more in line with expectations, since favorable reactions decrease sharply among subjects with more extreme positions. A clear explanation of these results is not available. Probably the inconclusive nature of the middle communication was a major factor (cf. Hovland and Mandell, 1952). For example, lack of conclusions in weighing the evidence may have increased the indecision of some subjects with moderate positions, while appearing to Republican supporters as consistent with the campaign strategy of their party in 1956 of resting "on the record" and "getting out the vote."

OPINION SHIFT FOR GROUPS WITH DIFFERING STANDS ON THE ISSUE

The final analysis of the results of the two communication studies concerns the likelihood of an individual being changed in his opinion by a communication. Here again we handle the results in terms of the subject's latitudes of acceptance-rejection and the discrepancy between the position of communication and the subject's stand. The individual's stand is viewed as an internal anchor. The attempted introduction of a standard (communication) far removed from the subject's stand would not be expected to affect his ratings of items as acceptable or unacceptable in any appreciable way. The standard would not be accepted. On the other hand, a standard close to his own position might be assimilated into the range of positions considered acceptable. Thus we should expect the following relationship to obtain:

With small discrepancies between the position of communication and that of the subject, changes of opinion in the direction advocated by communication will occur. With large distances between the stands taken in communication and by the subject, opinion changes will be infrequent. Changes in the direction opposite to that advocated by communication will be more frequent when the discrepancy between the stands taken in communication and by the subject is large.

Before proceeding to the discussion of our own results on this problem, some of the prior studies in the literature will be briefly reviewed.

Prior Studies

In several investigations the amount of change toward a communication has been determined for subjects with initial positions at varying distances from the communication. Let us first consider communication on social issues with some motivational relevance for the individual. An experiment by Ewing (1942) is sometimes cited as evidence that greater discrepancies between initial opinion and the position of communication produce greater change toward the communication. The issues in this experiment were not neutral ones. For example, one concerned the "native ability" of Negroes and another concerned capital punishment. Careful study of the report casts some doubt upon evidence for the conclusion that greater discrepancies are associated with greater change. Correlations are presented as evidence between amount of opinion change and the difference between initial opinion and communication. Those correlations range from .44 to .53. However, correlations of .48 and .56 were obtained between original opinion and amount of change for control subjects who received no communication. In view of Ewing's comment that the distributions of opinion scores were not at all normal and of the possible ceiling effects which might produce a spurious relationship, the evidence does not appear convincing.

On the other hand, when subjects judged the communication as "biased," "not logical," "opposed to experience," and "of doubtful reliability," their average initial opinion was considerably farther from the position of communication than that of subjects who judged the communication favorably (Table 4, p. 73). Subjects who judged the communication unfavorably (and whose initial opinion was farther from the communication) consistently shifted less, on the average, than individuals who viewed the communication favorably (Table 7, p. 76). In this experiment, some change away from the position of communication was reported for subjects with initial opinions close to the *perceived* position of communication. Ewing notes that this result was apparently produced by suspicions of the intent of the communication, since it did not occur when the intent was openly stated in the communication.

Despite his statement that large discrepancies between initial opinion and communication are associated with greater change, Ewing noted definite limitations on the correlation. "If . . . there is present a resistance to the propaganda material, the correlation will tend to disappear, for such resistance is itself, in part, a function of the amount of difference between the propagandist's opinion and that of the subject" (p. 84). Shifts away from communication, which are associated with resistance, were found to persist more than shifts toward communication. Ewing's interpretation was that negative shifts involved "a greater proportion of the self or of the personal regions" (p. 87).

In a study designed to compare the effects of informative and authoritative communication on individuals who scored high or low on a measure of "authoritarian personality" (F scale), Wagman (1955) reported that "authoritarian subjects" changed *away* from a communication presenting favorable information about Negroes. Likewise "nonauthoritarian" subjects changed *away* from communication urging intensification of prejudice and attributed to military and business leaders. In view of the correlations obtained between scores on the F scale and measures of prejudice, it seems likely that the initial stands of both "authoritarian" and "nonauthoritarian" subjects were located near the extreme opposite to that advocated in communication.

In an experiment utilizing the same issue, Carlson (1956) obtained a curvilinear relationship between frequency of attitude shift toward a pro-Negro communication and initial attitude on the issue. "The S's at the moderate positions

(positions 2, 3, and 4) were found to be significantly influenced by the experimental procedure, while extremely
prejudiced (position 1) and extremely nonprejudiced (positions 5 and 6) persons were not found to change systematically." (p. 259). The small proportion of change among nonprejudiced subjects is easily explained, since they already
agreed with the position advocated. The measuring instru-
ment did not permit subjects at the most prejudiced position
to shift away from communication; the most common finding was no change.

A related finding is reported by Tannenbaum (1956) who
concluded that "susceptibility to change is inversely proportional to the intensity of initial attitude." In this experiment,
source and communication were varied in a factorial design.
Since the measure of intensity was a summed score on six
evaluative scales, these results might be interpreted as indicative of the importance of the subject's stand and its personal
significance to him.

The effects of a discrepancy between the individual's stand
and the position advocated in communication have also been
investigated when the attitude pertains to a group norm and
the source of communication is a representative of the group.
There is considerable evidence that communication which
makes the individual aware that his stand deviates from a
norm of his reference group results in shifts toward the norm
by the deviant member (e.g. Gorden, 1952; Lau, 1954). It is
clear, however, that the extent of shift would depend on
the importance of the norm in the group, the individual's
position in the group, and several other factors.

The Prohibition and Election Studies

It will be recalled that in the first session of the prohibition study latitudes of acceptance and rejection were obtained for a small group of wet subjects, several groups of
dry subjects, and an unselected sample of college students,

most of them moderately wet. From one to three weeks later, arrangements were made through a member of the group being exposed to present a communication to each group. A wet (repeal) communication was presented to extreme dry subjects. A dry (prohibition) communication was presented to extreme wet and unselected subjects. A moderately wet communication (at about F position of the statements ranging from A to I) was presented to wet, dry, and unselected subjects.

The communications were of equal length, each requiring about fifteen minutes for delivery by tape recording. The arguments were those actually used by proponents of prohibition and repeal during the referendum campaign. Arguments in the three communications were arranged in the same order, but from the viewpoint of the different proponents. For example, each communication considered the religious aspect, the moral aspect, the health aspect, and financial aspects, but with quite different conclusions on the basis of the points marshaled in support of the advocated stand.

In Table 6 results are presented in terms of the percentage of subjects who changed their latitudes of acceptance in the direction advocated by communication, in the direction opposed to it, or who did not change. The net change column represents the differences between those changing in the direction advocated by communication and those who changed in the opposite direction. The net change is greater among the unselected group than among the drys when a wet communication is presented (p < .04). It will also be seen that the amount of change produced among the drys by a moderately wet communication (at F) is greater than that produced by the more extreme wet communication (at H). The net proportion changed by the former is 12 per cent, while it is only 4 per cent for the latter. This difference, however, is not statistically significant, and in any case it is difficult to establish that the two different communications were inherently equivalent in persuasiveness.

It will be noted that by confining our comparisons to groups who were initially selected as having known differences in their stand on the issue, we were able to avoid the regression effects often found in studies where amounts of

TABLE 6. *Opinion change: percentage of subjects changing in direction of communication or in opposed direction. (From Hovland, Harvey, and Sherif, 1957.)*

Subjects	N	Change in direction of communication	No change	Change in direction opposed to communication	Net change
		Wet communication (H)			
Drys	69	27.5	49.3	23.2	+4.3 *
Unselected	92	52.2	23.9	23.9	+28.3 *
		Dry communication (B)			
Wets	25	24.0	56.0	20.0	+4.0
Unselected	87	40.2	33.4	26.4	+13.8
		Moderately wet communication (F)			
Drys	114	31.6	49.1	19.3	+12.3

* Difference between changes: $p < .04$ (one tail).

change are compared for groups differentiated solely on the basis of initial scores on the attitude measure. Under the latter conditions those with more extreme scores often regress toward the mean, and this can either obscure the effect or produce a relationship artifactually.

Finally it will be noted from Table 6 that the predominant response among subjects holding extreme positions is to remain uninfluenced by communication. Even when subjects in these groups were influenced, shifts were seldom found in the item checked as best representing their own position. Instead, there was typically only an increase in the number

of other statements intermediate between their own positions and that of the communication which they would
check as "also acceptable."

The election issue. The general procedures in the second
session of the election study parallel those of the prohibition
study just summarized. The session started with presentation of one of the three communications by tape recording.
Each communication was about fifteen minutes in length
and covered the major issues of the campaign in the same
order, for example, the record of the major parties in pros-
perity, government efficiency, labor, agriculture, taxation,
education, natural resources, and so on. Points actually made
in the platforms of the major parties and the speeches of
their proponents were used. It will be recalled that one communication was strongly pro-Republican, one was strongly
pro-Democratic, and one presented both sides without drawing definite conclusions. A total of 86 subjects heard the pro-
Republican communication, 140 heard the pro-Democratic
communication, and 91 heard the middle communication.

The subjects' ratings of the nine statements on the election
issue in session 1 and in session 2 were compared. Because
the period of the study was marked by almost hourly appeals by the major parties through mass media, meetings,
and personal contacts, the changes in ratings can hardly be
attributed solely to the fifteen-minute communications introduced in session 2, in spite of the fact that the time interval
between sessions 1 and 2 was only one or two days. We can
be concerned here only with clear patterns in the direction
of shift for subjects with stands at varying distance from the
position advocated.

In view of the intensive campaign activity at the time, it
is of interest that nearly half of the 317 subjects who took
part in both sessions made no changes in their latitudes of
acceptance and slightly over 67 per cent checked the same

statement as most acceptable. Only one subject actually changed sides from Republican to Democrat. Ten subjects moved from the middle (E position) to a partisan stand, and another eight subjects changed from a moderately partisan stand to the middle position. Changes in the latitudes of acceptance were largely confined to the addition or elimination of a single position.

The analysis revealed similar frequencies of change for subjects whose stands differed from the positions of the pro-Republican or the pro-Democratic communication to the same extent. For our present purposes, therefore, the subjects exposed to these two extreme communications are combined in terms of the relative discrepancy between the subject's stand and the position advocated in communication. For example, extremely pro-Republican stands (represented by statements A and B) are most remote from the Democratic communication, while extremely pro-Democratic stands (H and I) are most remote from the Republican communication. In terms of our hypothesis, both may be combined as "extreme stands farthest from the position advocated in communication." Moderate stands may be combined as "moderate stands *far* from communication" and "moderate stands *near* communication." (For example, F and G positions are far from the Republican communication, and C and D are far from the Democratic communication.) Subjects who checked statement E are classified in the middle category.

Table 7 gives the percentages of subjects whose stands differ with respect to their relative distance from the position advocated by the two extreme communications, and whose latitude of acceptance shifted toward communication, away from communication, or did not change. The net change column gives the differences between the percentage changing in the direction advocated and that changing in the opposite direction. It will again be noted that the characteristic response of subjects with the extreme positions farthest from the communication is to remain unchanged.

Changes in the latitude of acceptance are more frequent for moderately pro-Republican (C, D) and moderately pro-Democratic (F, G) subjects. Subjects with moderate positions change more frequently toward a communication advocating an extreme position *near* their own and away from a position *remote* from their own. This pattern of shift was found in separate analysis of the pro-Republican and pro-Democratic communications as well. The differences in change for subjects with moderate stands near communica-

TABLE 7. *Opinion change for subjects exposed to pro-Republican and pro-Democratic communications: per cent of changes in mean acceptable statement for subjects whose initial stands differed by varying amounts from the position of extreme communications.*

Subject's stand	N	Change in direction of communication	No change	Change in direction opposed to communication	Net change
Extreme stands *farthest* from communication	82	20.8	60.9	18.3	+2.5
Moderate stands *far from* communication	61	22.9	45.8	31.3	−8.4 *
Middle (E)	20	30.0	45.0	25.0	+5.0
Moderate stands *near* communication	35	37.1	48.5	14.4	+22.7 *

* Differences between changes: $p < .05$.
(18 subjects already agreeing with the communication are omitted.)

tion and those with moderate stands remote from communication are significant.

The pattern of directions of opinion change produced by varying discrepancies between the subject's stand and the stand of communication lends support to our hypotheses. The difference between proportions of subjects with extreme stands and those with moderate stands who changed and who did not change the position checked as most acceptable is also highly significant (p < .001). To some extent, this difference may result from the ceiling imposed by statements at the extreme. However, only fourteen subjects initially checked the most extreme statements as most acceptable and three of them actually did change. The remaining subjects with extreme stands were free to change in either direction. Since the same tendency appears when either the most acceptable position or the mean acceptable position is employed, the conclusion that subjects with extreme stands are less likely to change in response to communication seems

TABLE 8. *Opinion change for subjects exposed to moderate communication: changes in mean acceptable statement for subjects whose initial stands differed slightly and widely from the middle communication*

Subject's stand	N	Change in direction of communication	No change	Change in direction opposed to communication	Net change
Extreme stands farthest from communication	51	15.6	58.8	25.6	−10.0
Moderate stands near communication	33	39.4	33.3	27.3	+12.1

(7 subjects with initial stands at E are omitted.)

warranted. The predicted boomerang effects for extreme discrepancies were not manifested.

Results for the middle communication are less clear. The trends support the main hypothesis concerning discrepancy between subjects' stands and the position of communication, although the differences in change are not significant. Table 8 presents the percentage of subjects whose stands were most remote from the middle communication (pro-Republican at A or B and pro-Democratic at H or I) and whose stands were closer to communication (C, D or F, G). The net change for subjects with positions near the middle communication was toward the position advocated, while net change was away from communication for subjects with more remote stands (A, B or H, I). Most of the subjects with extreme positions who were exposed to the middle communication were actively engaged in partisan political activity. Their change scores do not reveal regression effects and support the proposition that subjects with extreme positions are less likely to change. Only the difference between the proportions of subjects with extreme positions and with moderate positions who change and who do not change is significant ($p < .03$).

Opinion Shift on Less Ego-Involving Issues

The preceding experiments dealt with social issues which are highly involving for partisans of a pro or con position. The results revealed less frequent change with greater discrepancies between the individual's initial stand on the issue and the position of communication.

These findings may be compared with other recent experiments reporting increased shift with greater discrepancies between the subject's initial position and the communication. For example, Goldberg (1954) reported greater conformity to judgments attributed to an experimental group as the discrepancy between initial judgments and the standard increased. A similar conclusion by French (1956) was based on an unpublished study by French and Gyr. Such results are fairly typical in judgment of dimensions conducive to a wide margin of error, such as extent of autokinetic movement or personal characteristics judged from photographs, particularly if the source of the standard has positive value for the subject. However, even in highly unstructured situations, increasing amount of shift with larger discrepancies occurs only within limits. Whittaker's experiment reported in Chapter 3 demonstrates that the relationship breaks down in judgments of autokinetic movement when divergence between the subject's position and the standard is extreme.

We conclude that the magnitude of the range of assimilation, where opinions shift toward an introduced standard, is in part a function of the dimension of judgment. However, the differential shift exhibited by subjects in response to the same communication on a controversial issue which was reported in the last sections requires additional explanation. Our hypotheses concerning the reciprocal relations between the subject's own stand and the communication, in which the relative discrepancy between the two is a major parameter, were formulated for this purpose.

The individual's stand on a highly controversial social issue becomes a main anchor for his appraisal of communication on the issue when his stand has personal, hence motivational, significance. It is this ego-involvement with one's stand on an issue which limits the range of assimilation for other positions. If this analysis is correct, the range of assimilation should be more extensive with a lower degree of ego-involvement. An experiment by Hovland and Pritzker (1957) fulfills the requirements to test this proposition by using issues no more ambiguous than those in the election and prohibition studies but less ego-involving than the latter.

The Hovland and Pritzker experiment investigated the change in opinion on topics of a rather neutral nature produced by communications advocating new positions differing in varying degrees from the old. The communication consisted of the presentation of the opinion of respected leaders on various issues by means of check marks. This stems from the well-known procedure used by Arnett et al. (1931) and subsequently by several other investigators. The position of the communicator was located at varying distances from the position held by the subject. For example, subjects might be asked how many hours of sleep per night are needed for good health. Those who thought eight hours of sleep a night are adequate could be told that doctors consider nine or ten hours, or seven or six hours, best. Three separate communication items were employed. One advocated an opinion slightly different from the one held initially by the individual, one advocated a moderately different position, and a third presented a greatly different view.

Opinion questionnaires were administered and a month later a second questionnaire containing the communication items was presented. Seven degrees of agreement-disagreement were available, varying from "agree strongly" to "disagree strongly." The subject was asked to check the category which most nearly expressed his opinion toward statements on twelve topics. On the first questionnaire an additional item was included to secure subjects' selections of groups with particular authority on each topic. Results were tabulated and the group with the highest preference was used as the authority in the later communication.

The second questionnaire was administered a month after the first. Along with each opinion item, the position held by the chosen authority group was indicated. This opinion served as the communication and was varied systematically according to the subject's initial position.

Thus, in this experiment, communication was unequivocal and was attributed to a highly respected source. The topics were not calculated to have high motivational relevance to the subjects. The main results are presented in Table 9. The

TABLE 9. *Mean opinion change score with three strengths of communication. (Data from Hovland and Pritzker, 1957.)*

| | Degree of change advocated | | |
	Slight	Moderate	Marked
Positive communication	.89	1.33	1.57
Negative communication	.87	1.18	1.92
Combined	.88	1.25	1.75

$$p < .03 \qquad p < .05$$
$$p < .00001$$

results for the group for whom the advocated opinion differed slightly from the subject's own position are indicated in the left-hand column, those where the difference was moderate in the second column, and those where the difference was marked in the third column. It will be observed that the greater the deviation—in other words, the more discrepant the amount of change advocated—the greater the shift toward the communication.

Relative to the amount of change advocated, the obtained amount of change decreases as the discrepancy between initial opinion and communication increases. The authors report that for the slight discrepancy, 88 per cent of the change attempted was obtained. For the moderate discrepancy, the proportion is 62 per cent, and for the marked discrepancy it is 59 per cent.

Ego-Involvement and Attitude Change

Through comparison of results on the controversial prohibition and election issues with those on issues which were motivationally neutral, it is our conclusion that a strong stand on an issue which is personally involving for the individual functions as an anchor in his judgments and renders him less likely to be affected by highly discrepant, persuasive communication on the issue. In our research on social issues, ego-involved subjects have been obtained from groups actively supporting a particular stand on the issue. Since groups aligned on opposing sides rather infrequently adopt a moderate point of view on the topic, the most involved subjects in our research tended to be those with more extreme stands. Doubtless there are individuals committed with equal intensity to a position in the middle segment on an issue. The relationship underlying extremity of stand and commitment in our research is empirically determined by subject selection.

In the present development of research on social attitudes, the operational definition of commitment or ego-involvement on an issue in terms of active membership in groups advocating a given stand may be the most efficient in the long run. Some investigators prefer to attempt manipulations of personal involvement through experimental procedures linking the individual's performance on an opinion rating with another unrelated goal, such as showing up well as a research subject to the experimenter and other subjects. Such procedures are useful when the independent variables (instructions or procedures) bear some demonstrable relationship to the dependent variable and the research topic, e.g. instructions that the results of the subject's performance on an intellectual task will be placed on the college

records when the dependent variable is an achievement measure or the subject's evaluation of his performance.

However, when the stimulus material pertains to a social
issue, instructions and procedures which sensitize the individual to the experimental situation and his role as a subject
may mask any importance which his opinion on the issue
might have for him outside of the laboratory. The only pure
laboratory manipulation of involvement as a factor in change
of opinion on a social issue would have to start with a topic
of which the subject had never heard.

The objection to the operational criterion of group membership for personal involvement on the grounds that it con-
founds differences in information, social support, etc. seems
less serious than those which can be raised concerning dis-
regard for the personal importance of the issue coupled with
experimental procedures which add new difficulties in interpretation. For example, in Zimbardo's study of opinion
change on juvenile delinquency (1960) differential "involvement" was produced by instructions concerning the relation
of performance to the subjects' "values and personality."
The credibility of the situation was enhanced further by
attributing communication to a good friend who had also
been rated "expert" on another task. These procedures
surely sensitized the college girls who served as subjects to the
immediate aspects of the situation, but they could also mask
antecedent commitments on the issue. While the probabili-
ties of a delinquency case reported in an experiment being
of vital concern to college girls are low, the one "unexpected
finding" reported in this study would indicate that the subjects did differ in regard to their involvement with the issue.
In line with the finding that less involved individuals accept
more positions and reject fewer than highly involved individuals, Zimbardo reports that "those Ss who conformed
initially accepted a wider range of statements and rejected a

narrower range than did the nonconformers, i.e. they had larger latitudes of acceptance and smaller latitudes of rejection" (p. 91). This result is not easily reconciled with Zimbardo's additional report that subjects exposed to the highly involving instructions (who changed more) rejected more items than subjects in the less involving experimental condition, and suggests that considerable confounding of variables occurred.

Perhaps in selecting independent variables for research on social attitudes, it would be well to take stock with an eye to real life events. It is from this point of view that identification of ego-involved subjects in terms of active support of groups taking a stand on an issue seems valid. Also from this point of view, our predictions seem to gain support, in comparison to those which predict increasing change with increasing discrepancy between attitude and communication. Surely a communication advocating integration of schools in a community embroiled in opposing it is not likely to arouse much change in the direction of the communication, even if it comes from a prestigeful member of the community.

Concluding Remarks

Our present effort is to link judgment processes underlying reaction to communication with established findings from the experimental study of judgment. Judgment of communication precedes shifts in the individual's position as a consequence of exposure to it.

In earlier chapters certain regularities in the direction of shifts in judgment were noted as a function of the discrepancy between the stimuli being judged and the location of anchoring stimuli. Small discrepancies resulted in shifts toward the anchor ("assimilation effect"), while large discrepancies produced shifts away from the anchor ("contrast effect"). Anchorages for judgment may be located in the stimulus field, or they may be *internal*. In most social situations, judgment occurs relative to both external and internal anchors.

In response to a communication on a social issue, an internal anchor is involved if the individual has an established attitude on the issue. An attitude is inferred from characteristic categorical reactions, and attitude change is revealed by alterations of these characteristic reactions. When an attitude is associated with the individual's conception of himself in relation to his social world, communication relevant to it situationally produces ego-involvement. When an individual is thus ego-involved, his stand becomes a main anchor for evaluation. The individual does not regard the communication neutrally. The effects of communication presenting a widely divergent position are unlikely to be those intended. The individual is likely to judge the communication unfavorably and to be uninfluenced by it, as our experiments on controversial issues demonstrated. Another possibility, which was evident in reactions to extreme communications on the political campaign, is that the highly involved individual may move still further away from a divergent communication. He retrenches, so to speak, by taking a stand more opposed to the communication than the one he initially upheld.

On the other hand, opinions on issues ordinarily arousing less ego-involvement are subject to more change by communications presenting widely different stands. Hovland and Pritzker's study demonstrated greater change with wide differences between initial opinion and communication. Communication is more effective in producing shifts, and change away from communication is infrequent.

The research findings in this chapter suggest the utility of our research orientation toward reaction to communication and opinion change. The bare essentials of the problem of when change occurs and the *direction* of change in response to communication were formulated in terms of the discrepancy between the individual's stand on the issue and the stand presented in the communication. Specific research can be designed to investigate the effects of differing relationships between the individual's stand (internal anchor) and a communication (external anchor). In the preceding chapter we proposed that for this purpose the individual's stand on a controversial issue may be conceived as a range of positions on the issue (latitude of acceptance) which is accompanied by categorical rejection of other positions (latitude of rejection). An indicator of the latitude of acceptance proved fruitful in analysis of the results of our experiments. Research concentration on latitudes of acceptance and rejection gives promise of greater coherence to the study of reaction to communication and attitude change.

It is readily apparent that both the individual's stand and a communication may vary in several respects other than the relative discrepancy between the two positions. The study of interaction among several factors, operating simultaneously as they do in an actual communication situation, is a formidable task requiring refined experimental design and analysis. The relationship between the stands of the individual and the communication would seem to be focal for relating other factors involved in attitude change to the underlying judgment processes.

Other factors which clearly would seem to affect reaction to communication and the direction of attitude change can be mentioned. The stands of different individuals vary in their personal significance and in the size and locations of the latitudes of acceptance and rejection. The communication, in turn, may vary in many respects other than the position it advocates. It may also vary with respect to the clarity with which this stand is presented and whether its intent is obscured or clearly identified. The communication may be rather factual or it may be highly persuasive. It may involve deeply cherished stands, convictions, or ideals other than those with which it explicitly deals. The source of communication may be anonymous or highly authoritative. It may be presented by a representative of one's reference group or by a member of an antagonistic out-group. The topic of the communication (which is the object of the individual's attitude) may be clearly perceptible (e.g. the climate of one's geographic region) or it may involve abstract conceptualizations on a subject whose truth or falsehood is beyond the individual's reach (e.g. the future of space travel).

This brief enumeration suggests the value of focusing for a time on a boundary relationship and then proceeding in easy steps through possible variations. In the long run, this orientation promises coherence of research findings on reaction to communication and better understanding of the general processes underlying attitude change.

CHAPTER 8

Summary and Implications

THIS BOOK IS primarily concerned with the analysis and clarification of processes of judgment when an individual reacts to the type of stimulus material exemplified by communications advocating a stand on a social issue. The present approach developed from our conviction that the study of attitude problems would profit from an attempt at specific articulation with established findings from experiments on judgment. Various psychophysical methods are examined and their results compared in order to derive leads for an understanding of the relationships between the arrangements of stimuli involved in these procedures and the psychological processes operative under each. At the same time, pertinent indications of the more recent experimental developments in the study of attitude, emotion, personality characteristics through "cognitive processes" are analyzed. It is our aim to relate these two lines of work on judgment to each other and to utilize the results in developing research on attitude and communication problems.

NATURE OF PSYCHOPHYSICAL RESEARCH

Psychophysical studies of judgment are concerned with the rating of one stimulus in relation to another stimulus or series of stimuli. The subject's task is to identify differences between stimuli on the basis of some physical attribute,

177

such as weight, length, or pitch. Two different types of judgment study may be distinguished in terms of their objectives. In the first, the investigator is concerned with determining *discriminative capacity* for a particular sense modality; in the second he is concerned with analyzing the *placement* or *categorization* of particular stimuli in a series. These two objectives are of course intimately related, since placement always involves capacity to discriminate. But they are by no means equivalent. The type of judgment with which we are most concerned is the process of placement. Only when displacements may be attributable to lack of ability to discriminate among the alternatives need we inquire into the first problem.

Experiments primarily concerned with assessment of discriminative capacity are typically designed to provide conditions which minimize the possibility of distortions or systematic displacements produced by individual bias. On the other hand, experiments on placement may deliberately utilize stimulus arrangements which allow displacements, in order to study the internal factors which produce systematic displacements. Fundamentally, these differences are a matter of emphasis, since some discrepancy between psychological (subjective) and physical (objective) scale positions is bound to occur in any study of judgment. Different stimulus conditions and different rating methods, however, are known either to increase or to decrease the likelihood of systematic displacement according to the opportunity provided for factors such as "set," past experience, and motives to come into play. When attitudes toward individuals or issues are involved, judgments concerning individuals or issues are bound to be affected by such factors.

LEADS FROM JUDGMENT STUDIES

The following generalizations from studies of judgment of simple sensory stimuli summarize the principal phenomena and relationships which we have utilized in proceeding to the social area:

An individual confronted with a series of stimuli tends to form a psychological scale for judgment, even when the stimulus series is not well graded and when explicit standards for judgment are lacking. Henceforth, judgment of a related stimulus is made in terms of the categories of this reference scale.

The nature of the judgment scale is determined to an important extent by the conditions under which it is formed. Some differences in scales formed under different stimulus arrangements and varying procedures in laboratory experiments are noted in the following illustrations of modal types:

A. *To the extent that the psychological scale for judgment is formed on the basis of an unambiguous stimulus series with well-graded stimulus differences and with explicit objective anchors within the series, the correspondence between stimulus values and judgment values is relatively close.* In the classical psychophysical experiments using the method of constant stimuli, the stimuli constitute a well-graded series and are presented to the subject one at a time with a "standard," which serves as the anchor. The subject judges the variable stimuli in terms of the standard, and it is found that he is able to do so with considerable correspondence between stimulus values and judgment values. Subjective bias is at a minimum.

B. *To the extent that a stimulus series lacks explicit standards, the judgment scale is less stable and placement is less accurate for those stimuli located in the segment of the series remote from the end stimuli.* Experiments using the method

of single stimuli have shown that the introduction of an explicit standard by the experimenter is not essential for the
formation of a judgment scale. When a stimulus series is
presented in which well-graded stimuli are to be judged
without an explicit standard, a psychological scale develops
which also corresponds, on the whole, to the range and
relative positions of the stimulus values in the series. However, at first the scale is apt to be highly variable. It is also
less accurate for the placement of those stimuli remote from
the end stimuli, since the latter tend to serve as anchors in the
absence of explicit standards provided by the experimenter.
An increased opportunity for systematic displacement is
thus provided, particularly in the middle segment, by eliminating an explicitly designated standard.

C. *To the extent that both objective standards and a
graded series of stimuli are lacking, the contributions of internal factors (including set) and social influences (including
instructions) to the formation of a judgment scale are increased.* Even when stimuli are not well graded in the dimension being judged and no explicit standard is presented,
some type of categorization occurs. This is shown for example
in judgments of the extent of perceived movement in the
autokinetic situation. Here an individual establishes a range
and mode of judgment on the basis of internal factors and of
relevant external stimuli, including social influence and instructions. Even in this highly ambiguous situation, the categorization process is limited by objective conditions, such as
the distance between the subject and the stimulus and the
exposure time of the stimulus.

*When the individual has had little prior experience with a
graded stimulus series and is furnished no explicit standard
for judging it, the end values of the series initially serve as
anchors (or reference points) in establishing the scale.* In
weight-lifting experiments, for example, the heaviest and

lightest weights are identified early and thus end points of the judgment scale are established. Other stimuli are judged according to their perceived position relative to the end points. As stated by Volkmann (1951), judgments are most variable and most likely to deviate from the objective stimulus values in the middle segment of the stimulus series; thus he concluded that "it is primarily the *end-stimuli* that control the oscillations of the absolute scale" (p. 283). Results of representative experiments are discussed in Chapter 3. The uncertainty about intermediate positions is general and shows up in related measures, such as reaction time and degree of confidence with which judgments are rendered.

Anchoring stimuli introduced by the experimenter within or without the stimulus series significantly affect the way the individual places the series stimuli. An anchor located *within* the range of a stimulus series facilitates the judgment of items in that segment. The introduction of anchors considerably above or below the stimulus range has the effect of constricting judgments of stimuli within the series to a few categories of the judgment scale located farthest from the anchor position (Chapter 3).

In the new experiments reported in this volume, it is shown that the relative distance between the anchor and the stimulus series is a crucial determinant of displacement. An anchor placed *at either end* of a series, or even *slightly above* or *slightly below* the series, will produce an *assimilation effect*. Thus judgments are displaced in the direction *toward* the anchor. However, if the anchor is removed progressively further from the series so that it lies *considerably above* or *considerably below* the end stimuli, a *contrast effect* ensues. Judgments are displaced *away* from the anchor, causing a decrease in items judged as near the anchor and an increase in items placed in categories at the opposite end of the scale.

Various factors may interact with the position of an anchor, affecting the extent of the assimilation or contrast effects obtained. One of these is the range of the stimulus series: whether the stimulus series is wide or narrow in extent. Some experimental indication of the influence of this variable is presented in Chapter 3.

Assimilation and contrast effects produced by different anchor conditions are also obtained in judgments of dimensions lacking in objective structure. As mentioned above, experiments using the autokinetic effect have shown that subjects tend to form categories for judging under these conditions which bear some relation to objective conditions (time of exposure, size of room, distance from stimulus) and that variability of judgment decreases over time. The introduction of an explicit anchor, in the form of another person's judgment, is found to affect judgment in predictable directions. An anchor located near the limits of the psychological scale produces an assimilation effect: judgments are shifted in the direction of the anchor. The range of anchor locations in which assimilation occurs is greater for judgments of such unstructured dimensions than for judgments of well-graded stimuli. However, an anchor sufficiently remote from the subject's scale does not result in assimilation. There may be a tendency for displacement of judgments away from the anchor.

Anchorages may be internal as well as external. The effect of internal anchors was first shown for judgments of angles of visual inclination, where instructions to the subject to establish a gauge in his own mind caused shifts in placement. Similar effects of internal anchors produced by instructions have been shown for affective judgments (Chapter 4). When the individual has an established reference scale, composed of categories of acceptance and rejection, his own stand at some position on the scale is likely to function as anchor in his judgments of various characteristics of the stimuli. This extension of anchoring effects is a principal problem of the new experiments in this book dealing with placement of verbal items and communications on social issues. The extension requires consideration of learning factors, since a stand relative to social materials is a product of learning. Again we start with experiments using simpler materials.

Learning, i.e. the conditions and extent of past experience with the stimulus material, is an important determinant of the nature of an individual's judgment scale and his placements of relevant stimuli (Chapter 4). This is shown most clearly in the experiments of Tresselt, where the placements of weights by subjects (such as professional weight lifters) having prior experience with heavy objects or by subjects with differing amounts of practice in the experiment were markedly different from those of subjects lacking such prior experiences. Past experience in the form of practice provides the subject with an established reference scale which affects his placement of relevant stimuli.

The establishment of a reference scale in which a certain category acquires a higher value for the subject than others has been accomplished in the laboratory through rewards. In this case, the valued category functions as an internal anchor in subsequent judgments of related items and in the absence of reward. For example, lines of intermediate length were displaced toward a longer category which had been rewarded. The extent to which internal anchors affect placement depends, however, on the nature of the stimulus situation. The more ambiguous the set of stimuli presented, the greater the effect of internal anchors. Conversely, with well-structured stimulus materials, less displacement owing to subjective reference points is likely.

Implications for Internalization of Anchors

The conditions under which social anchors are effective in modifying judgment have implications for the process by which individuals internalize categories which are social in origin. The greater the stimulus ambiguity or the difficulty of the task, the greater the effectiveness of socially provided anchors. Social "suggestion" which conflicts with the subject's established attitudes or his prior experience with the task is markedly less effective. Internalization of the suggested placement occurs when such conflicts are not prominent.

Likewise, the internalization of a social anchor depends upon the subject's prior placement of the *source*. Prior experience may lead the individual to regard the source as lacking in credibility and to reject his suggestion. He is more likely to heed the suggestion of a source he has come to regard as expert, authoritative, or prestigeful. In actual social interaction, the source is frequently identified by the subject as a member with given standing in his group or in an out-group. The effectiveness of a suggestion is thus closely related to the individual's motivational ties with his reference groups and the relative standing accorded other individuals and groups in their established scheme of relationships.

Some of the internal anchors mentioned above may be experimentally produced through prior success or failure and through a set provided by specific instructions for the task. They differ from the more lasting internal anchors which are formed during the previous life experiences of the subject and situationally aroused in the experiment. The latter include the individual's established attitudes toward the stimulus material and the degree of his ego-involvement with it.

In a number of experiments, an established attitude has been shown to produce systematic and predictable variations of judgment. When the stimulus material is relevant to the subject's intense attitudes, the task of judging it situationally involves his attitudes even though the instructions were not intended to arouse them. If the stimulus material is also ambiguous in nature, his placements are apt to err systematically in directions predictable from his established acceptances or rejections of the items. In this case, even though the task calls for the objective ordering of the items, his ego-involvement with the material results in placements correlated with his established categories of acceptance–rejection. For example, the placement of skin color by a Negro judge is closely related to the judge's liking or disliking of the person whose skin color he is rating.

APPLICATIONS TO SOCIAL JUDGMENT

In dealing with simple sensory material it is possible to arrange stimuli on a physical dimension and to study the relationship between the stimuli and judgments about them. However, in studying judgment of social stimuli, particularly verbal formulations of social issues, we do not usually have physical units in terms of which to order the stimuli. In this case, social reality is a guide as to how other individuals in the culture at a given time define the issue and what the extremes are. One could thus describe the scales with which social psychologists are most concerned as *psychosocial* to distinguish them from the *psychophysical* ones investigated by physiological and sensory psychologists.

As with simple sensory stimuli, there is a tendency for individuals to order attitudinal material despite the fact that the stimuli may not be clearly graded and that an explicit standard may be lacking (Chapter 5). In placing verbal items representing stands on a social issue, individuals are apparently capable of discriminating among statements which represent the diverse positions of different social groups, and of ordering these statements on a continuum with respect to some dimension, such as the "favorableness-unfavorableness" of the items to their object.

The nature of the stimulus material affects the difficulty or ease of this task. Some statements are indicative of definite social stands, and there is considerable agreement as to their scale position. Other statements may be ambiguous or express ambivalence or indifference. For most social issues, the extreme positions appear to be more clearly stated and more easily recognized than positions located between the extremes.

Thus an individual confronted with the task of placing items by the method of equal-appearing intervals is likely to orient his appraisal of various positions primarily in terms of the extreme positions, particularly if he is not intimately acquainted with all stands on the issue. Placement of intermediate items is more variable. This situation would account for the well-known greater variability of middle positions on attitude scales constructed on the basis of this procedure.

However, if the individual has a strong attitude on the issue, his placement of a given attribute of the items, for example their favorableness-unfavorableness, is likely to be influenced by his own acceptance and rejection of the item's content. Particularly in placing ambiguous items, his own stand on the issue constitutes an anchor for judgment of scale positions. The result is marked displacement of intermediate items as a function of the subject's stand on the issue under consideration. In Chapter 5 a series of experiments is reported in which items initially used by Hinckley on the issue of the social position of the Negro were judged by various subjects whose stands on the issue were known. Subjects ranged from groups with anti-Negro attitudes to those with pro-Negro views, including a number of Negro groups.

It was found that subjects whose stands on the issue corresponded to a position between the extreme segments sorted items by the method of equal-appearing intervals in such a manner that the key items were more or less equally spaced along a continuum. On the other hand, Negro judges and white judges with markedly pro-Negro views, tended to displace the items in middle positions toward the opposite extreme and away from the central positions. This outcome is in clear opposition to Thurstone's assumption that the placement of an item by a judge is independent of the judge's own stand on the issue. The results are apparently not caused by lack of ability to discriminate between the items, since it was also shown by Kelley, Hovland, Schwartz, and Abelson (1955) that subjects with extreme stands on the issue were able to discriminate between the same items when the paired-comparisons method was employed.

The degree of displacement of middle-position items may be so marked that only a limited number of categories are utilized. This is most clearly illustrated by allowing subjects free choice in selecting the number of categories which they regard as necessary to make appropriate distinctions between the different positions on the issue. Highly involved subjects holding extreme positions use fewer categories than more neutral subjects. These same subjects with extreme positions tend to neglect certain categories when required to sort the items in a larger number of prescribed categories in the equal-intervals procedure. They tend to see an issue as black or white.

The displacement of items under equal-intervals procedures, even by subjects with extreme views on the issue, is a function of the ambiguity of the statements and the considerable number of statements presented for scaling. In our studies using a large number of items, the clearly stated ex-

treme items were not displaced. By reducing both the ambiguity and the number of items, it was shown by Prothro
that displacements are substantially reduced.

With complex verbal items which are more easily interpreted in alternative ways, there is a similar tendency for displacement to occur as a function of the subject's own stand
on the issue. If a communication presenting a stand between
the clearly defined extremes is given to subjects with varying
positions on the issue, those whose stand corresponds most
closely to it tend to place the communication correctly. Some
subjects with positions slightly removed from that of the
communication may judge it more like their own position
than it actually is (assimilation effect), while those subjects
whose positions are more remote will displace the communication's stand away from their own (contrast effect). The greater
the discrepancy between the subject's own stand and the position advocated in the communication, the greater the contrast effect. Furthermore, there is a marked tendency to
evaluate a communication as fair or unbiased when it advocates a stand closely approximating that held initially by
the subject. Communications are judged as unfair, however,
when they advocate a position diverging markedly from the
subject's stand. These results are summarized in Chapter 7.

The results discussed so far are derived from experiments
in which the subject is asked to place items in terms of
different objective positions on the issue, and not to give his
personal view nor to judge the items in terms of his agreement
or disagreement with them. His task corresponds more closely
to that of psychophysical experiments in which the subject
places sensory stimuli in appropriate categories of weight,
brightness, or loudness. The two situations differ, however, in
that in judging the social material those individuals with established attitudes have an internal reference scale for judg-

ment in which certain categories are rejected and others are accepted.

A somewhat different procedure is involved when the individual is asked to make affective judgments as to how well he likes certain stimuli or whether he agrees or disagrees with verbal statements. Here he is required to make his own preferences explicit and his own position is automatically being evaluated. Most of the studies of affective judgment have used stimulus materials such as colors and odors which are not highly ego-involving for most subjects.

In our studies of the prohibition and election issues, we proceeded to study the distribution of evaluative judgments of attitudinal items in order to determine the positions which the subject accepts, those which he rejects, and those about which he is noncommittal (Chapter 6). This was done to learn about the established reference scales which individuals bring to the task of ordering relevant items. Our results may be briefly summarized:

When a subject is given a series of attitudinal items covering a range of positions from one extreme to the other, and is asked to indicate those he accepts and those he rejects, a characteristic pattern is obtained in which there is a region of acceptance, a region of rejection, and frequently a noncommittal region between the two. For the highly ego-involving issues with which we have been concerned, the latitude of rejection is characteristically broader than the latitude of acceptance.

The relative sizes of the latitudes of acceptance and rejection are shown to be related to the individual's own preferred stand on the issue, and therefore not completely fortuitous. Individuals with more extreme positions tend to have broader segments of rejection and narrower latitudes of acceptance. Furthermore, individuals holding extreme views tend to have broader latitudes of rejection than persons with moderate views. This finding specifies one consequence of a relationship reported in earlier investigations between extremity of position and intensity of stand. It also provides an explanation for the results discussed above on categorization of items with many or few gradations of opinion by ego-involved or neutral subjects. Provision must also be made, however, for the occasional individual who strongly upholds a position in the middle segments and rejects positions at the extremes.

We infer that few subjects with extreme positions can tolerate alternative views on the issue, at least when the topic is highly ego-involving. The reference scale of acceptance-rejection, with its narrow latitude of acceptance and wide latitude of rejection, is reflected in the categorization of items according to their favorableness and unfavorableness on the issue: intermediate items fall within the latitude of rejection and are lumped together in the extreme category opposite to the individual's own stand. On the other hand, persons with views intermediate to the extremes have narrower latitudes of rejection which ordinarily include both of the extreme positions. Remaining positions are characterized either by acceptance or at least by a noncommittal attitude.

If we are dealing with an issue toward which the subject has no established or strong attitude, we can expect the latitude of acceptance to be broad and, accordingly, a communication to have a good chance of being assimilated to it. But if we are dealing with a strongly held position, particularly at the extremes, we should expect that the communication would be rejected unless it is quite close to the individual's own stand on the issue. If it is not, we may even expect a reaffirmation of the individual's stand so that it becomes more difficult to influence him after he has been repeatedly presented with a position discrepant from his own. These and other implications are discussed in the next section.

Implications for the Effects of Communication

The effects of a communication are found to depend upon the manner in which it is categorized by the individual. This judgment process involves the concerted operation of a number of determinants, whose prominence varies in different conditions. Some of the principal determinants have been discussed, including stimulus arrangements, characteristics of the material judged, the availability of external or internal standards, familiarity, and certain motivational factors.

Distance separating positions of communicator and recipient. A primary factor influencing the effect of a communication is the relative distance between the stand of the individual and the position advocated in the communication. This distance is not adequately defined by the discrepancy between the single position which the individual finds most acceptable and the position of communication as measured by some outside criterion such as social consensus. The distance referred to is defined by the individual's placement of communication at some position (near or distant) relative to his own stand on the issue. We have found that the individual's own stand includes a range of acceptable positions and is accompanied by a latitude of rejection. Thus the effect of a communication depends upon the placement of communication relative to the individual's latitudes of acceptance and rejection.

The latitudes of acceptance and rejection vary with degree of familiarity, the extremity of the individual's stand, and the degree of ego-involvement with the issue—whether it arouses an intense attitude or, rather, whether the individual can regard the issue with some detachment as primarily a "factual" matter.

It is our contention that the distance between the position of the communication and that of the recipient can only be assessed through knowledge of the judgment scale of the recipient. What appear to be small differences in position to one individual (say the difference between the Russian and Chinese concerning the nature of communism as it appears to a typical American "democrat") may be of enormous significance to the other individual. Thus where there are small distances on a scale for one individual there may be tremendous ones for another. Combined with these distances are clear-cut differences in the intensity with which the beliefs are held, specified by latitudes of acceptance and rejection. It is on the basis of these phenomena that individuals frequently misjudge the difficulty involved in changing another's opinion: what seems to them only a minor revision may be to the person they are attempting to influence a major shift in stand.

Degree of familiarity. When first confronted with the task of judging unfamiliar material, the individual places stimuli into a very few undifferentiated categories. Initially, the stimuli may simply be named, as in the case of trainees in aircraft recognition who are equipped at the outset of training with only the category "airplane." In categorizing unfamiliar material, stimulus characteristics are initially dominant. Thus, if the extreme items of a series are definite, they rather quickly acquire an anchoring function. If, however, salient anchors are not provided by stimulus characteristics, categorizations provided by other individuals are particularly likely to be adopted. The influence of another person's judgment in initial exposures to the autokinetic situation is an example.

The individual who lacks information does not make fine differentiations among the various positions on an issue. He places items into undifferentiated categories bearing some resemblance to pronounced stimulus characteristics or to categorizations provided by others. Examples of these tendencies may be found in many fields. The novice to the political arena may distinguish a communist from a capitalist, but may lump everyone into these two categories without regard for the various shadings of political opinion. The beginner in the field of personality analysis may classify individuals into polar types provided him—extrovert and introvert—before discovering a host of finer distinctions.

The results presented in the volume *Order of Presentation in Persuasion* by Hovland et al. (1957) concerning the relative effectiveness of material presented first as compared with material presented second have a bearing here. One generalization occasionally encountered is that primacy is far more effective on new issues than on old ones. This can be explained readily in the present terms. When a new issue is presented, the communication has an important influence in structuring and defining its nature. It is a case of establishing the relevant anchors, and with unfamiliar materials external stimulus determinants tend to carry more weight. Hence the communication which reaches the individual first plays a dominant role. When the individual has had considerable prior familiarity with the issue, however, the impact of the first communication in structuring the issue is greatly lessened. Here the individual's familiarity with the range of positions on the issue determines his placement of particular stands. If he has taken a stand on the issue, it is more powerful than external anchors, hence the order of presentation is likely to be much less significant. With familiarity the role of internal factors overrides this stimulus aspect.

With relative lack of familiarity, categories of acceptance and rejection are rather undifferentiated owing to the lack of an intensely held stand. For purposes of change through communication, the situation is favorable. A communication presenting further information and a definite point of view should not encounter any great resistance. Findings on opinion change with exposure to more or less neutral (nonego-involving) materials should be equally applicable to unfamiliar issues, for the individual has not yet formed differentiating categories of acceptance and rejection. Such issues are not yet matters of great importance to the individual, although they may subsequently become so.

The individual's own stand and degree of ego-involvement. The individual who has taken a strong stand at some extreme position on an issue may, as we have seen, also place items into a few categories. However, the determinants of placement bear quite different relationships, and the difference is apparent in the effects of communication diverging from his own stand. In categorization, his own stand provides the major anchor, specific items being placed within his latitude of acceptance or outside of it in rejected categories. Thus, even a moderate communication may be placed in an extreme category if it is sufficiently ambiguous. The person with a strong stand in a highly involving issue may judge a communication as within his own camp or against it, despite familiarity with the nuances of opinion held by those whose views are opposite to his. Thus, unless stimulus arrangements and the task compel him to discriminate the delicately shaded differences of opinion, he lumps them into a single category or into a very few categories at the pole opposite his own position.

For purposes of attitude change, the difference between this situation and the broad categorization of unfamiliar issues lies in the operation of an established reference scale consisting of accepted and rejected segments. In the case in point, the latitude of acceptance is very narrow and the latitude of rejection broad. Here, the problem of changing the individual's position through communication is exceedingly difficult. Even a communication designed to present a moderate point of view may be regarded by the recipient with an extremely "pro" stand as being somewhat "con" in its approach. The advocated position falls squarely within his latitude of rejection and, far from convincing him, the communication is more likely to reinforce his own entrenched stand.

A possibility for producing change through communication might be that of stating a position which differs so slightly from the individual's own position that it falls at the limits of his latitude of acceptance or perhaps within a noncommittal area between the latitudes of acceptance and rejection. These circumstances are conducive to an assimilation rather than a contrast effect: instead of being regarded as much further removed from the subject's stand than it actually is, the communication is assimilated and placed closer to the individual's position than it is in fact. In this way the limits of the latitude of acceptance might be expanded slightly to include the few new divergent points of the communication. Conceivably, in such small doses, the holder of an intense position might be gradually shifted.

Another device which may be used by the communicator would be to compare the position he advocates with one even more extreme, thus making the difference between his position and that held by the recipient appear smaller. Under some conditions at least one would anticipate that the introduction of stimuli at a point extremely removed from that held by the communicatee would serve to make the positions of communicator and recipient appear more similar and hence increase the likelihood of change through communication.

Not every familiar issue is highly ego-involving for every individual. The issue may be one on which he does not take a strong stand or his stand is not a matter of much personal significance. On the basis of our findings for subjects with moderate and neutral positions on social issues, we are led to expect that latitudes of acceptance are broad for issues that are not appreciably ego-involving for the individual. Latitudes of rejection, in turn, would be quite narrow. For issues which are not the objects of intensely held attitudes, we would expect this broad latitude of acceptance no matter what position the individual finds most acceptable.

Thus a person's position on an issue that is not highly ego-involving can be shifted more readily than a stand on an ego-involving issue which is the object of an established attitude. A broad latitude of acceptance makes the former case promising for opinion change. This is a plausible explanation of the findings by Hovland and Pritzker that the greater the discrepancy between opinion and a message on issues regarded as "factual," the greater the change in opinion.

As a brief summary of the above implications, we may say that the wider the latitude of acceptance for positions on an issue, the greater the probability of producing opinion change through communication. In addition, the greater the ego-involvement with an issue on which the individual has an established attitude, the narrower the latitude of acceptance and, consequently, the less the likelihood of opinion change through communication.

A serious methodological problem is that of specifying exactly the kind of involvement(s) of the subject in reacting to a stimulus item and in performing the task set by the experimenter. It is one thing to get the subject involved in the task through the experimenter's instructions or through his attaching great importance to his performance in the experiment. It is quite another thing for the subject to be involved in reacting to the stimulus items or in performing the task because the item or the task itself is related to an issue important to his very conception of himself. The first kind of involvement is situationally aroused, viz. through instruc-

tions by the experimenter, the significance of his participa-
tion in the particular experiment, the consequences of the
outcome of his performance. The second kind is aroused
through the intrinsic importance for him of the issue to which
the item or task is related because it concerns his abiding
stand on an issue. It is ego-involvement of this second kind,
aroused by a stimulus item related to his stand on an issue, by
a person or group to whom the individual is committed, that
is of special interest in the area of attitude measurement and
attitude change. Unfortunately it is extremely difficult to
manipulate the latter type of involvement experimentally.
Thus at present our theorizing is primarily with respect to
the effects of high involvement achieved naturalistically
through life experiences. It may not apply to the variation
produced through laboratory attempts to modify involvement
by heightening of interest or attempts to produce temporary
commitment. Thus we may find what appears to be a curvilinear relationship between the effects of communication
and the experimentally induced involvement. If only small
degrees of change are produced through manipulation we
may primarily be seeing the effects of heightened interest
and of increased attention to the communication and these
may produce greater opinion change. Only when powerful
modifications are made will the predicted resistance to
change and "boomerang" effects become apparent. It is our
belief that the changes produced by Zimbardo (1960) were
primarily of the first variety and that those studied correla-
tionally in the Hovland-Sherif (1952), Sherif-Hovland (1953)
studies were of the latter type.

Illustrative Areas of Application

Voting. This formulation is consonant with the results presented by a number of investigators on the effects of communication on voting. These studies, notably those of Lazarsfeld,

Berelson, and others, have tended to show how little modification is produced in political position by the mass media. We
have seen that on issues which are highly ego-involving, positions much removed from the individual's own stand fall
primarily within his latitude of rejection. Hence they are
practically ignored and may under some circumstances even
increase the individual's commitment to his own stand. This
is akin to intensification or "reinforcement effect" in voting
studies. For only a small number of individuals, typically
those slightly removed from the position of communication,
will there be attitude change. Thus "conversion" based on
exposure to communication is a relatively infrequent phenomenon.

On less vital, more superficial issues, of the type dealt with
in many opinion surveys, the role of the mass media may on
the other hand be tremendous. In this case, as we have seen,
there will typically be a broadened latitude for acceptance
and a relatively narrow range of rejection. Thus, with issues
which are not deeply involving, marked changes may be
expected, particularly when the source is placed by the individual in a highly favored category (e.g. expert, authority
figure, prestigeful figure, etc.). Studies of voting behavior
also bear out this implication. It has been repeatedly found
that the "independent voter" is not the man with mastery of
the issues who is undecided as to the preferable alternative
but is rather the individual without much knowledge of the
issues who is more readily swayed by political arguments
than those who already have more information on the nature
of the issues and have a clear-cut preference.

There is a temptation to overgeneralize concerning the
relative ineffectiveness of communication on ego-involving
issues and to extend the conclusions beyond the conditions
under which the studies in question were carried out. In the
voting issue mentioned above, the communications through

mass media probably do not convey factual evidence of over-whelming weight in favor of or against the political parties involved (Republican or Democratic). They are primarily attempts at persuasion in which similar arguments are hurled back and forth without the support of incontroverti-ble factual evidence. Consequently, the factor of personal influence, not communication, tips the balance in these cases. We should, however, make room for those cases in which communication through mass media conveys events of crushing proportions. The announcement of the attack on Pearl Harbor by radio and newspapers, reaching millions of people at the same time, was certainly effective in chang-ing the political attitudes of a good many individuals in the matter of isolationism. Conceptually, the case may be akin to the readjustment of the psychological scale following exposure to compelling external stimuli which brings the judgment scale and stimulus series into closer correspon-dence.

Stereotype. Studies of stereotypes and stereotyped thinking may be cited as another area of application. A stereotyped view of an ethnic group, for example, implies a categoriza-tion process wherein a group in its entirety is placed in a single category on a scale of acceptance-rejection or su-periority-inferiority. Associated with the category is a limited selection of attributes which are tenaciously affirmed to de-pict that group in its entirety. Thus the attributes associated with groups placed in acceptable categories are predomi-nantly favorable. Attributes associated with rejected groups are largely unfavorable.

Stereotyping is particularly prevalent when learning oc-curs in the absence of extensive contact with the stimulus and is based largely on categorical verbal formulations by others. This may be the case whether the stereotype pertains to an emotion-laden issue like relations between groups or to a neutral topic. In his recent systematic experiments, W. R. Hood (1961) has verified the relatively greater strength of concept or generalization formed through dictum or formula over concept or generalization built up by the individual inductively, i.e. through specific encounters with the common element of the stimuli in question. In other words, stereotypes learned chiefly "by formula" may be ego-involving or they may represent poorly differentiated categories with little motivational significance.

To the extent that ego-involvement is lacking, increased contact with a range of stimulation or more information could be expected to result in more finely differentiated categories. When a broad categorization rests on a strong attitude, however, contact or information diverging from the individual's conceptions is unlikely to alter the picture substantially.

Scaling. The results on latitudes of acceptance and rejection have implications concerning the character of psychological scales. During recent years a number of criticisms have been made of the assumptions underlying unitary scales of measurement, as formulated by Guttman and others. The present results tend to support some of these criticisms. They would indicate that on controversial social issues which are ego-involving, there is not a psychological continuum on which an individual who accepts a given stand also accepts all less extreme positions. This is particularly clear in the results in Chapter 6. Many individuals with stands near an extreme position rejected other positions both more extreme and less extreme than their own. The results strongly suggest that individuals do not perceive such social issues in the manner required by the assumptions of unitary cumulative scales. Unlike categorization in *psychophysical* scales where cumulative scales are applicable, the categories of *psychosocial* scales represent discontinuous segments.

SUGGESTIONS FOR FURTHER RESEARCH

Some of the areas in which the study of judgment illumi-
nates the problems of attitude and opinion change have been
indicated in this volume. The evidence cited indicates conceptual and methodological advantages to be gained by
studying attitude problems through processes of judgment.
It is clear, however, that judgment processes are inextricably
related to basic problems of learning, motivation, perception, concept formation, and social values or norms. These
vast problem areas could be mentioned only briefly as they
pertained to our main theme. As a result, we faced great
gaps, some of which we shall now mention briefly.

Judgment and language. An important area for research
lies in relating the study of judgment to that of language.
Language constitutes a framework within which concepts
develop. Studies in the area of social judgment frequently
use words as stimuli to be categorized. What are the effects
of different verbal forms on our interpretation of the stimuli
and judgment of them? What constitutes verbal ambiguity?
The extent to which distortions in interpretation result from
ambiguity may be closely related to the type of language
structure utilized.

The findings summarized in this volume indicate the importance of further study of the effects of anchors in verbal
form upon placement. The acquisition of word meaning itself implies a categorizing process. This was illustrated in
the brief discussion of stereotypes in the preceding section.
In forming a concept of the meaning of a word, the individual must place various possible meanings into those most
frequently used, those excluded, and several gradations in
the middle range. The process is probably closely related
to the degree of familiarity with the referent of the word;
lack of familiarity would limit the possibility of fine dif-

ferentiations. Many social categories or classifications are learned deductively, that is more by formula rather than by extensive contact with their referents. What differences obtain when acquisitions of such concepts is accompanied by formation of an intense attitude and when it is not?

Information and opinion. A closely related research area is the relationship between information and opinion. Either lack of familiarity or an intense attitude may produce errors in placement, although errors produced by the latter are ordinarily less amenable to shift through increased information. For research purposes it would be desirable to know more about the placements of positions on an issue by types of subjects having the following characteristics:

(a) Little information on an issue with no strong opinion.
(b) Little information but an intensely held opinion.
(c) Considerable information and yet no strong opinion.
(d) Considerable information and a strongly held opinion.

Degree of information affects the number of categories used for placement, as does strength of opinion. However, we would expect errors in a systematic direction only with an intense attitude. Do such displacements occur equally with poorly informed and well-informed individuals? Theoretically, individuals (c) and (d) should be able to make finer differentiations in view of their increased information. When the stimulus arrangements permit a varying number of categories, do placements made by individual (d) reflect his more constricted latitude of acceptance? How do his judgments differ from those of individual (b), who also has an intensely held opinion but has little information on the issue?

Latitudes of acceptance and rejection. The concepts of latitudes of acceptance and rejection may have important implications for further research. Our hypotheses involve the expectation that individuals with wide latitudes of acceptance will be influenced by communications to a significantly greater extent than those whose tolerance for other positions is restricted. A research test of this proposition is indicated. Since the individual's stand and the relative size of his latitude of acceptance are correlated (Chapter 6), it would be desirable to use subjects with relatively homogeneous positions. For example, one might obtain a large number of subjects with a moderate position but varying latitudes of acceptance, such as the two subtypes of middle-of-the-road subjects mentioned in Chapter 6. Are those who have a middle position but a narrow latitude of acceptance more apt to resist the influence of communications than those who also take a middle position but indicate a wide tolerance for other views?

For research purposes, latitudes of acceptance and rejection might be tied both to ego-involvement and to questions of habitual approaches to controversial issues and opinion situations.

Affective judgments. It is apparent that a great need in linking judgment study and investigations of attitude and attitude change is intensive research into judgment of affective and motivationally relevant material. To what extent is it possible to modify placements of the acceptance-rejection type, and how do these modifications transfer to other situations? What differences obtain in judgments of preference for color or odor and preference for human associates or another highly ego-involving matter? The findings in this volume would indicate that one major difference is that for the latter issues, the individual's established reference scale of acceptance-rejection includes categories perceived as his own stand. On such issues, the individual may be reluctant to disclose his preferences and rejections.

If so, research procedures and techniques which make him aware that his own stand is being investigated may produce artifacts.

"Indirect" measurement of attitudes. It is suggested that the distortions in placement produced by the individual's own stand can be utilized to study attitudes without direct interrogation of the subject. This possibility has hardly been explored. The results in Chapter 5 show that the distribution of scale values, as well as the choice of an appropriate number of categories for placement (the individual's "own" categories), are closely related to the individual's stand on an issue. A powerful "indirect" assessment method may thus be provided for attitude measurement. Further definitive research on this problem is needed.

Personality and judgment. In *Personality and Persuasibility* (Volume 2 in the present series), the personality characteristics of individuals showing varying degrees of susceptibility to persuasion are investigated. An interesting research question is how individuals with different personalities will categorize issues. One might employ the judgment-scaling type of approach to investigate differences in personality. This might be particularly interesting in developmental terms. Individuals of differing ages could be asked to sort opinion statements to determine their ways of viewing an issue. How many categories are used at different ages? Are the earlier categories broader and relatively undifferentiated, followed by a more differentiated reference scale? Does further experience tend to solidify the individual's position so that the relative sizes of the latitudes of acceptance and rejection change?

Utilization of ratio scales. In a recent review of L. L. Thurstone's collected papers (1959a) Stevens has raised the question as to whether it would not be possible to apply what he refers to as "direct" procedures to the measurement of attitudes and values, rather than to rely exclusively on the Thurstonian approach in which scale values are primarily derived from measures of discriminal dispersion, or variability. This suggests a promising area for research in social judgment, and some attempts to apply the direct approach based on assessment of the ratio between subjective values have been made in the measurement of economic values, or utility (Stevens, 1959b). But we must not expect that such procedures would make inapplicable the various considerations we have discussed throughout the present volume. There will still exist wide individual differences (as indeed simple sensory scaling by ratio methods shows) and the range of items, past familiarity with the issue, varying conceptions of the standard and of the subjective ratio (Stevens, 1960), and various motivational factors will still play a major role whenever we are dealing with the charged and personally relevant stimuli involved in everyday elicitation of attitudes. We will face many of the same problems despite the use of a different technique of scaling.

Ego-involvements, reference groups, and judgment scales. Attitude change is inextricably tied with motivational factors and the formation of judgment scales on the one hand, and with the developing conceptions of reference groups and social norms on the other. A major finding, it will be recalled, is that the position upheld by the individual on an ego-involving issue is relatively immune to change as a consequence of exposure to adverse communication. In fact, the more committed an individual is to a social issue, the more uncompromisingly entrenched he is likely to become in the face of adverse communications.

The stand upheld by the strongly committed individual is not just any position in a series of available positions. It is his *own* position. The individual does not indicate his own position in neutral terms; he states it in personal terms.

He asserts "I am a dry," "I am a Republican," "I am a Baptist." He perceives his stands as parts of what *he* is and what he claims to be, with appropriate motivational and emotional overtones. His personal identity and the stability of his conception of himself depend in no small part on the stability and perpetuation of his stands on so many issues of social life.

In short, the individual's own stands are motivational components in his psychological make-up. Expressions of irritation and feelings of hurt manifested by the individual in the face of appeals too alien to his own stand are evidence of this.

The motivational components referred to as "own stands" enter into the judgment process as major anchors which, in appropriate stimulus conditions, are major determinants of the categorization of relevant items. In this volume, "own stands" were studied mainly through their effects: for example, displacements of relevant stimulus items produced by them and the relative magnitudes of latitudes of acceptance and rejection for moderate as compared with extremely committed individuals.

But we have not traced the development of the individual's "own stands" in his particular life history. Of course an individual is not born a "wet" or "dry," anti-Negro or pro-Negro, "Republican" or "Democrat." In each case, he *becomes* one. The individual's own stand is a product of learning during his development.

In this connection, we encounter problems of the individual's reference groups. Reference groups may be characterized as the groups to which the individual relates himself or aspires to relate himself, and these constitute the principal sources from which his "own stands" on social issues are derived. The norms or values of his reference groups on a given issue may be represented as psychosocial scales with modal segments of approval and disapproval. Since the individual actively seeks acceptance and approval by his reference group, the psychosocial scales of the reference group become the individual's judgment scales, subject within limits to modifications produced by distinctive personality factors. Henceforth, the individual's categorization and, hence, his evaluation of an appeal (communication) are made in terms of this judgment scale.

Formulation of the problem of the relative immunity to change of stands on ego-involving issues in terms of the reference group concept and its derivatives (e.g. reference person or idol) has a definite methodological advantage. By linking the individual's judgment scales with his reference groups, a number of attitude and attitude change problems could be clarified and investigated through specifiable social and psychological indices. This approach would enable us to account for some effective cases of communication through the mass media and through personal influence.

It must be readily admitted that the study of problems of attitude and attitude change in terms of learned scales of judgment, anchors with motivational components, and reference groups is in its infancy. The exploration of interrelationships in these areas may hold the promise of comprehensive and integrated accounts of attitude problems.

REFERENCES

Italic numbers at the end of each reference refer to pages in the present volume.

ALPFR, T. G., 1946. Task-orientation vs. ego-orientation in learning and retention. *Amer. J. Psychol., 59*, 236–48. *21*

ARNETT, C. E., DAVIDSON, H. H., and LEWIS, HELEN H., 1931. Prestige as a factor in attitude change. *Sociol. Soc. Res., 16*, 49–55. *169*

ASCH, S. E., 1940. Studies in the principles of judgments and attitudes: II. Determination of judgments by group and by ego-standards. *J. Soc. Psychol., 12*, 433–65. *89, 90*

ASCH, S. E., 1952. *Social psychology.* New York, Prentice-Hall. *63, 87*

ASCH, S. E., 1956. Studies of independence and conformity: I. A minority of one against a unanimous majority. *Psychol. Monogr., 70*, No. 9. *76f., 87, 88*

ASCH, S. E., BLOCK, HELEN, and HERTZMAN, M., 1938. Studies in the principles of judgments and attitudes. I. Two basic principles of judgment. *J. Psychol., 5*, 219–51. *79f.*

BARRETT, M., 1914. A comparison of the order of merit and the method of paired comparisons. *Psychol. Rev., 21*, 278–94. *26*

BARTLETT, F. C., 1932. *Remembering: a study in experimental and social psychology.* Cambridge, Cambridge Univ. Press. *21*

BEAMS, H. L., 1954. Affectivity as a factor in the apparent size of pictured food objects. *J. Exper. Psychol., 47*, 197–200. *95*

BEEBE-CENTER, J. G., 1932. *The psychology of pleasantness and unpleasantness.* New York, Van Nostrand. *28*

BERKOWITZ, L., 1960. The judgmental process in personality functioning. *Psychol. Rev., 67*, 130–42. *72*

BOVARD, E. W., JR., 1948. Social norms and the individual. *J. Abnorm. Soc. Psychol., 43*, 62–69. *35, 87*

BOVARD, E. W., JR., 1953. Conformity to social norms in stable and temporary groups. *Science, 117*, 361–63. *90*

BRESSLER, J., 1933. Judgments in absolute units as a psychophysical method. *Arch. Psychol.*, No. 152. *31*

BROWN, D. R., 1953. Stimulus-similarity and the anchoring of subjective scales. *Amer. J. Psychol., 66*, 199–214. *50*

BRUNER, J. S., 1946. Social value and need as organizing factors in perception. *Amer. Psychol., 1,* 241. *21*

BRUNER, J. and RODRIGUES, J. S., 1953. Some determinants of apparent size. *J. Abnorm. Soc. Psychol., 48,* 17–24. *75, 95*

CAMPBELL, D. T., HUNT, W. A., and LEWIS, N. A., 1957. The effects of assimilation and contrast in judgments of clinical materials. *Amer. J. Psychol., 70,* 347–60. *72*

CANTRIL, H., 1938. The prediction of social events. *J. Abnorm. Soc. Psychol., 33,* 364–89. *80*

CARLSON, E. R., 1956. Attitude change through modification of attitude structure. *J. Abnorm. Soc. Psychol., 52,* 256–61. *159f.*

CARTER, L. F. and SCHOOLER, K., 1949. Value, need, and other factors in perception. *Psychol. Rev., 56,* 200–07. *75, 94*

CARTWRIGHT, D., 1941. Relation of decision time to the categories of response. *Amer. J. Psychol., 54,* 174–96. *130*

CHAPMAN, D. W. and VOLKMANN, J., 1939. A social determinant of the level of aspiration. *J. Abnorm. Soc. Psychol., 34,* 225–38. *81f, 83, 94*

CLARK, K. B., 1940. Some factors influencing the remembering of prose material. *Arch. Psychol.,* No. 253. *21*

COFFIN, T. E., 1941. Some conditions of suggestion and suggestibility: a study of certain attitudinal factors influencing the process of suggestion. *Psychol. Monogr.,* No. 241. *63, 87*

CONKLIN, E. S. and SUTHERLAND, J. W., 1923. A comparison of the scale of values method with the order-of-merit method. *J. Exper. Psychol., 6,* 44–57. *27*

CRUTCHFIELD, R. S. and EDWARDS, W., 1949. The effect of a fixated figure on autokinetic movement. *J. Exper. Psychol., 39,* 561–67. *34*

DAS, J. P., RATH, R., and DAS, R. S., 1955. Understanding versus suggestion in the judgment of literary passages. *J. Abnorm. Soc. Psychol., 51,* 624–28. *94*

DEUTSCH, M. and GERARD, H. B., 1955. A study of normative and informational social influences upon individual judgment. *J. Abnorm. Soc. Psychol., 51,* 629–36. *90*

DUKES, W. F. and BEVAN, W., 1952. Size estimation and monetary value: a correlation. *J. Psychol., 34,* 43–53. *75*

EDWARDS, A. L., 1946. A critique of "neutral items" in attitude scales constructed by the method of equal-appearing intervals. *Psychol. Rev., 53,* 156–69. *105*

EDWARDS, A. L., 1957. *Techniques of attitude scale construction.* New York, Appleton-Century-Crofts. *25, 27, 116*

EDWARDS, A. L. and KENNEY, K., 1946. A comparison of Thurstone and Likert techniques of attitude scale construction. *J. Appl. Psychol., 30,* 72–83. *102*

ERIKSEN, C. W. and HAKE, H. W., 1957. Anchor effects in absolute judgments. *J. Exper. Psychol., 53,* 132–38. *42, 61f.*

EWING, T. N., 1942. A study of certain factors involved in changes of opinion. *J. Soc. Psychol., 16*, 63–88. *158f.*

EYSENCK, H. J. and CROWN, S., 1949. Experimental study in opinion and attitude methodology. *Int. J. Opin. and Attit. Res., 3*, 47–86. *102f.*

FEHRER, E., 1952. Shifts in scale values of attitude statements as a function of the composition of the scale. *J. Exper. Psychol., 44*, 179–88. *111*

FERNBERGER, S. W., 1920. Interdependence of judgments within series for the method of constant stimuli. *J. Exper. Psychol., 3*, 126–50. *31*

FERNBERGER, S. W., 1931. On absolute and relative judgments in lifted weight experiments. *Amer. J. Psychol., 43*, 560–78. *31, 32, 33, 40*

FERNBERGER, S. W. and IRWIN, F. W., 1932. Time relations for the different categories of judgment in the "absolute method" of psychophysics. *Amer. J. Psychol., 44*, 505–25. *33f.*

FESTINGER, L., 1953. An analysis of compliant behavior. In M. Sherif and M. O. Wilson (eds.), *Group relations at the crossroads.* New York, Harper. *76*

FESTINGER, L., 1957. *A theory of cognitive dissonance.* Evanston, Row, Peterson. *3*

FISHMAN, J. A. and LORGE, I., 1954. The role of the culture-group affiliation of the "judge" in Thurstone attitude-scale construction. *Amer. Psychol., 9*, 368–69 (abstract). *112*

FRENCH, J. R. P., JR., 1956. A formal theory of social power. *Psychol. Rev., 63*, 181–94. *168*

GIBSON, J. J., 1950. *The perception of the visual world.* Boston, Houghton Mifflin. *22*

GILCHRIST, J. C. and NESBERG, L. S., 1952. Need and perceptual change in need-related objects. *J. Exper. Psychol., 44*, 369–76. *21*

GOLDBERG, S. C., 1954. Three situational determinants of conformity to social norms. *J. Abnorm. Soc. Psychol., 49*, 325–29. *167f.*

GORDEN, R. L., 1952. Interaction between attitude and definition of the situation in expression of opinion. *Amer. Sociol. Rev., 17*, 50–58. *160*

GRAHAM, C. H., 1958. Sensation and perception in an objective psychology. *Psychol. Rev., 65*, 65–76. *22*

GRANNEBERG, R. T., 1955. The influence of individual attitude and attitude-intelligence upon scale values of attitude items. *Amer. Psychol., 10*, 330–31 (abstract). *112*

GUILFORD, J. P., 1954. *Psychometric methods.* New York, McGraw-Hill, 2nd ed. *25, 47, 51*

HAMMOND, K. R., 1948. Measuring attitudes by error choice: an indirect method. *J. Abnorm. Soc. Psychol., 43*, 38–48. *95f.*

HANSCHE, J. and GILCHRIST, J. C., 1956. Three determinants of the level of aspiration. *J. Abnorm. Soc. Psychol., 53*, 136–37. *82f.*

HARVEY, O. J., 1953. An experimental approach to the study of status relations in informal groups. *Amer. Sociol. Rev.*, *18*, 357–67. *83*

HARVEY, O. J., 1956. An experimental investigation of negative and positive relations between small groups through judgmental indices. *Sociometry*, *19*, 201–09. *84*

HARVEY, O. J. and CAMPBELL, D. T., 1960. Judgments of weight as affected by adaptation range, adaptation duration, magnitude of unlabeled anchor, and judgmental language (mimeographed). *58ff.*

HEIDER, F., 1958. *The psychology of interpersonal relations*. New York, Wiley. *3*

HEINTZ, R. K., 1950. The effect of remote anchoring points upon the judgment of lifted weights. *J. Exper. Psychol.*, *40*, 584–91. *45, 46, 51*

HELSON, H., 1947. Adaptation-level as frame of reference for prediction of psychophysical data. *Amer. J. Psychol.*, *60*, 1–29. *29*

HELSON, H., 1948. Adaptation-level as a basis for a quantitative theory of frames of reference. *Psychol. Rev.*, *55*, 297–313. *29*

HELSON, H., 1959. Adaptation-level theory. In S. Koch (ed.), *Psychology, a study of a science*, Vol. 1. New York, McGraw-Hill, pp. 565–621. *29, 51*

HELSON, H. and NASH, M. C., 1960. Anchor, contrast, and paradoxical distance effects. *J. Exper. Psychol.*, *59*, 113–21. *57, 60*

HERSKOVITS, J. J., 1949. *Man and his works*. New York, Knopf. *36*

HEVNER, K., 1930. An empirical study of three psychophysical methods. *J. Gen. Psychol.*, *4*, 191–210. *26, 27*

HINCKLEY, E. D., 1930. Attitude toward the Negro Scale No. 3, Forms A and B (L. L. Thurstone, ed.). Chicago, Univ. of Chicago Press. *108*

HINCKLEY, E. D., 1932. The influence of individual opinion on construction of an attitude scale. *J. Soc. Psychol.*, *3*, 283–96. *102, 104, 109*

HINCKLEY, E. and RETHLINGSHAFER, D., 1951. Value judgments of heights of men by college students. *J. Psychol.*, *31*, 257–96. *92*

HOLLINGWORTH, H. L., 1914. Professor Cattell's studies by the method of relative position. In R. S. Woodworth (ed.), *Psychological researches of James McKeen Cattell. Arch. Psychol.*, *30*, 75–91. *27*

HOOD, W. R., 1961. Rigidity of concept utilization as a function of inductive and deductive derivation. Unpublished doctorate dissertation, Univ. of Oklahoma. *200*

HOOD, W. R. and SHERIF, M., 1961. Verbal report and judgment of an unstructured stimulus (in press). *77*

HOVLAND, C. I., 1951. Changes in attitude through communication. *J. Abnorm. Soc. Psychol.*, *46*, 424–37. *147*

HOVLAND, C. I., 1954. Effects of mass media of communication. In G. Lindzey (ed.), *Handbook of social psychology*. Cambridge, Mass., Addison-Wesley. *146*

HOVLAND, C. I., HARVEY, O. J., and SHERIF, M., 1957. Assimilation and contrast effects in reactions to communication and attitude change. *J. Abnorm. Soc. Psychol.*, *55*, 244–52. *131, 135, 150, 155, 162*

HOVLAND, C. I., JANIS, I. L., and KELLEY, H. H., 1953. *Communication and persuasion.* New Haven, Yale Univ. Press. *155*

HOVLAND, C. I., LUMSDAINE, A. A., and SHEFFIELD, F. D., 1949. *Experiments on mass communication.* Princeton, Princeton Univ. Press. *13*

HOVLAND, C. I. and MANDELL, W., 1952. An experimental comparison of conclusion drawing by the communicator and by the audience. *J. Abnorm. Soc. Psychol.*, *47*, 581–88. *156*

HOVLAND, C. I., MANDELL, W., CAMPBELL, ENID H., BROCK, T., LUCHINS, A. S., COHEN, A. R., McGUIRE, W. J., JANIS, I. L., FEIERABEND, ROSALIND L., and ANDERSON, N. H., 1957. *The order of presentation in persuasion.* New Haven, Yale Univ. Press. *193*

HOVLAND, C. I. and PRITZKER, H. A., 1957. Extent of opinion change as a function of amount of change advocated. *J. Abnorm. Soc. Psychol.*, *54*, 257–61. *168ff., 174, 196*

HOVLAND, C. I. and SHERIF, M., 1952. Judgmental phenomena and scales of attitude measurement: item displacement in Thurstone scales. *J. Abnorm. Soc. Psychol.*, *47*, 822–32. *2, 21, 104ff., 114, 197*

HUNT, W. A., 1941. Anchoring effects in judgment. *Amer. J. Psychol.*, *54*, 395–403. *7of.*

HUNT, W. A. and VOLKMANN, J., 1937. The anchoring of an effective scale. *Amer. J. Psychol.*, *49*, 88–92. *69f.*

JANIS, I. L., HOVLAND, C. I., FIELD, P. B., LINTON, HARRIETT, GRAHAM, ELAINE, COHEN, A. R., RIFE, D., ABELSON, R. P., LESSER, G. S., and KING, B. T., 1959. *Personality and persuasibility.* New Haven, Yale Univ. Press. *204*

JOHNSON, D. M., 1955. *The psychology of thought and judgment.* New York, Harper. *130*

JOURARD, S. M. and SECORD, P. F., 1955. Body-cathexis and the ideal female figure. *J. Abnorm. Soc. Psychol.*, *50*, 243–46. *85, 95*

KATZ, DANIEL (ed.), 1960. Attitude change. *Publ. Opin. Quart.*, spec. issue, *14*, No. 2, i–365. *3*

KELLEY, H. H., HOVLAND, C. I., SCHWARTZ, M., and ABELSON, R. P., 1955. The influence of judges' attitudes in three methods of scaling. *J. Soc. Psychol.*, *42*, 147–58. *114ff., 187*

KELMAN, H. C., 1950. Effects of success and failure on "suggestibility" in the autokinetic situation. *J. Abnorm. Soc. Psychol.*, *45*, 267–85. *66, 78*

KLEIN, G. S., SCHLESINGER, H. J., and MEISTER, D. E., 1951. The effect of personal values on perception: an experimental critique. *Psychol. Rev.*, *58*, 96–112. *95*

KNOWER, F. H., 1935. Experimental studies of changes in attitudes: I. A study of the effect of oral argument on change of attitude. *J. Soc. Psychol., 6,* 315–47. *146f.*

KUBANY, A. J., 1953. A validation study of the error-choice technique using attitudes on national health insurance. *Educat. Psychol. Measurem., 13,* 157–63. *96*

LAMBERT, W. W. and LAMBERT, P. E. C., 1953. Some indirect effects of reward on children's size estimations. *J. Abnorm. Soc. Psychol., 48,* 507–10. *75*

LAMBERT, W. W., SOLOMON, R. L., and WATSON, P. D., 1949. Reinforcement and extinction as factors in size estimation. *J. Exper. Psychol., 39,* 637–41. *75*

LA FAVE, L. and SHERIF, M., 1959. Placement of items on a controversial social issue. Institute of Group Relations, Univ. of Oklahoma (mimeographed). *123, 140f.*

LAU, J. B., 1954. Attitude change as related to change in perception of the group norm. *Dissertat. Abs., 14,* 1108. *160*

LEVINE, J. M., CHEIN, I., and MURPHY, G., 1942. The relation of intensity of a need to the amount of perceptual distortion. *J. Psychol., 13,* 283–93. *21*

LONG, L., 1937. A study of the effect of preceding stimuli upon judgment of auditory intensities. *Arch. Psychol.,* No. 209. *31, 40, 45, 47, 60*

LUCHINS, A. S., 1944. On agreement with another's judgment. *J. Abnorm. Soc. Psychol., 39,* 97–111. *63, 87*

LUCHINS, A. S. and LUCHINS, E. H., 1955. On conformity with true and false communications. *J. Soc. Psychol., 42,* 283–303. *76f., 87*

MANIS, M., 1960a. The interpretation of opinion statements as a function of recipient attitude. *J. Abnorm. Soc. Psychol., 60,* 340–44. *123, 153*

MANIS, M., 1960b. The interpretation of opinion statements as a function of message ambiguity and recipient attitude. Unpublished manuscript. *153*

MANIS, M., 1960c. The interpretation of opinion statements as a function of recipient-attitude and source prestige. Unpublished manuscript. *153f.*

MANSKE, A. J., 1937. The reflection of teachers' attitudes in the attitudes of their pupils. In G. Murphy, L. B. Murphy, and T. M. Newcomb, *Experimental social psychology.* New York, Harper. *147*

MARKS, E., 1943. Skin color judgments of Negro college students. *J. Abnorm. Soc. Psychol., 38,* 370–76. *21, 91f., 127*

MAUSNER, B., 1953. Studies in social interaction: III. Effect of variation in one partner's prestige on the interaction of observer pairs. *J. Appl. Psychol., 37,* 391–94. *89*

MAUSNER, B., 1954a. The effect of prior reinforcement on the interaction of observer pairs. *J. Abnorm. Soc. Psychol., 49,* 65–68. *78*

MAUSNER, B., 1954b. The effect of partner's success in a relevant task on the interaction of observer pairs. *J. Abnorm. Soc. Psychol., 49,* 557–60. *89*

MAUSNER, B., 1960. The effect of an instructed bias on judges in a Thurstone scale construction. Graduate School of Public Health, Univ. of Pittsburgh (unpublished paper). *113, 124*

MAUSNER, B. and BLOCH, B. L., 1957. A study of the additivity of variables affecting social interaction. *J. Abnorm. Soc. Psychol., 54*, 250–56. *79*

McCORD, F., 1948. The formation of group norms in waking suggestion. *J. Soc. Psychol., 27*, 3–15. *87*

McGARVEY, HULDA R., 1943. Anchoring effects in the absolute judgment of verbal materials. *Arch. Psychol.*, No. 281. *45*

McGREGOR, D., 1938. The major determinants of the prediction of social events. *J. Abnorm. Soc. Psychol., 33*, 179–204. *80*

MOORE, H. T., 1921. The comparative influence of majority and expert opinion. *Amer. J. Psychol., 32*, 16–20. *89, 90*

MOOS, M. and KOSLIN, B., 1952. Prestige suggestion and political leadership. *Publ. Opin. Quart., 16*, 77–93. *95*

MURPHY, G., MURPHY, LOIS B., and NEWCOMB, T. M., 1937. *Experimental social psychology.* New York, Harper. *146*

NASH, MYRTLE C., 1952. A quantitative study of effects of past experience on adaptation-level. *Dissertat. Abs., 12*, 335–36. *69*

NEEDHAM, J. G., 1935. Rate of presentation in the method of single stimuli. *Amer. J. Psychol., 47*, 275–84. *33*

OGBURN, W. F., 1922. *Social change.* New York, Viking Press. *36*

OGBURN, W. F., 1955. *Technology and changing family.* Boston, Houghton Mifflin. *36*

PARDUCCI, A., 1954. Learning variables in the judgment of single stimuli. *J. Exper. Psychol., 48*, 24–30. *50f., 69, 85*

PARDUCCI, A., CALFEE, R. C., MARSHALL, LOUISE M., and DAVIDSON, LINDA C., 1960. Context effects in judgment: adaptation level as a function of the mean, midpoint, and median of the stimuli. *J. Exper. Psychol., 60*, 65–77. *42f.*

PEAK, HELEN, 1958. Psychological structure and psychological activity. *Psychol. Rev., 65*, 325–47. *70*

PERLOE, S. I., 1960. Status and judgment of occupational prestige. Unpublished paper. *71f., 82*

PFAFFMAN, C., 1935. An experimental comparison of the method of single stimuli and the method of constant stimuli in gustation. *Amer. J. Psychol., 47*, 470–76. *32*

PINTNER, R. and FORLANO, G., 1937. The influence of attitude upon scaling of attitude items. *J. Soc. Psychol., 8*, 39–45. *102, 103*

POSTMAN, L. and MILLER, G. A., 1945. Anchoring of temporal judgments. *Amer. J. Psychol., 58*, 43–53. *45, 51, 56f.*

PROSHANSKY, H. and MURPHY, G., 1942. The effects of reward and punishment on perception. *J. Psychol., 13*, 295–305. *21, 74*

PROTHRO, E. T., 1955. The effect of strong negative attitude on the placement of items in a Thurstone scale. *J. Soc. Psychol., 41,* 11–17. *112*

REESE, E. P., REESE, T. W., VOLKMANN, J., and CORBIN, H. H., 1953. *Psychophysical research—summary report* (1946–1952). Mount Holyoke College, Psychophysical Research Unit (lithoprint). *41, 43f., 86*

REMMERS, H. H., 1938. Propaganda in the schools: do the effects last? *Publ. Opin. Quart., 2,* 197–210. *146*

ROGERS, S., 1941. The anchoring of absolute judgments. *Arch. Psychol., 37,* No. 261. *44f., 46, 52, 56*

ROHRER, J. H., BARON, S. H., HOFFMAN, E. L., and SWANDER, D. V., 1954. The stability of autokinetic judgments. *J. Abnorm. Soc. Psychol., 49,* 595–97. *35*

ROSENBERG, M. J., HOVLAND, C. I., McGUIRE, W. J., ABELSON, R. P., and BREHM, J. W., 1960. *Attitude organization and change.* New Haven, Yale Univ. Press. *4*

ROSENTHAL, B. G. and LEVI, J. H., 1950. Value, need, and attitude toward money as determinants of perception. *Amer. Psychol., 5,* 313 (abstract). *95*

RUSSELL, D. H. and ROBERTSON, I. V., 1947. Influencing attitudes toward minority groups in a junior high school. *School Rev., 55,* 205–13. *147*

SANFORD, R. N., 1937. The effects of abstinence from food upon imaginal processes: a further experiment. *J. Psychol., 2,* 145–59. *21*

SECORD, P. F., BEVAN, W., and KATZ, B., 1956. The negro stereotype and perceptual accentuation. *J. Abnorm. Soc. Psychol., 53,* 78–83. *80f.*

SHERIF, M., 1935. A study of some social factors in perception. *Arch. Psychol.,* No. 187. *34, 35, 63*

SHERIF, M., 1936. *The psychology of social norms.* New York, Harper. *76, 87*

SHERIF, M., 1937. An experimental approach to the study of attitude. *Sociometry, 1,* 90–98. *76, 87*

SHERIF, M., 1947. Some methodological remarks related to experimentation in social psychology. *Int. J. Opin. and Attit. Res., 1,* 70–93. *47, 58*

SHERIF, M., 1948. *An outline of social psychology.* New York, Harper. *46, 91*

SHERIF, M., 1960. Some needed concepts in the study of social attitudes. In J. G. Peatman and E. L. Hartley (eds.), *Festschrift for Gardner Murphy.* New York, Harper, pp. 194–213. *128*

SHERIF, M., HARVEY, O. J., WHITE, B. J., HOOD, W. R., and SHERIF, CAROLYN W., 1961. *Intergroup Conflict and Cooperation: The Robbers Cave Experiment.* Norman, University of Oklahoma Book Exchange, pp. 140–47. *84*

SHERIF, M. and HOVLAND, C. I., 1953. Judgmental phenomena and scales of attitude measurement: placement of items with individual choice of number of categories. *J. Abnorm. Soc. Psychol., 48,* 135–41. *2, 118ff., 197*

SHERIF, M. and SHERIF, CAROLYN W., 1953. *Groups in harmony and tension.* New York, Harper. *125*

SHERIF, M. and SHERIF, CAROLYN W., 1956, rev. ed. *An outline of social psychology.* New York, Harper. *46, 128, 146, 147*

SHERIF, M., TAUB, D., and HOVLAND, C. I., 1958. Assimilation and contrast effects of anchoring stimuli on judgments. *J. Exper. Psychol., 55,* 150–55. *51ff.*

SHERIF, M., WHITE, B. J., and HARVEY, O. J., 1955. Status in experimentally produced groups. *Amer. J. Sociol., 60,* 370–79. *83*

SHIBUTANI, T., 1955. Reference groups as perspectives. *Amer. J. Sociol., 60,* 562–69. *91*

SINHA, D., 1952. An experimental study of a social factor in perception: the influence of an arbitrary group standard. *Patna Univ. J.,* Jan.–April (reprint). *87*

SPERLING, H. G., 1952. An experimental study of some psychological factors in judgment. Summarized in S. E. Asch, *Social psychology.* New York, Prentice-Hall, pp. 487–90. *63*

SPIVAK, M. and PAPAJOHN, J., 1957. The effect of the schedule of reinforcement on operant conditioning of a verbal response in the autokinetic situation. *J. Abnorm. Soc. Psychol., 54,* 213–17. *78*

STEVENS, S. S., 1951. Mathematics, measurement, and psychophysics. In S. S. Stevens (ed.), *Handbook of experimental psychology.* New York, Wiley, pp. 1–49. *25*

STEVENS, S. S., 1959a. *Sic transit gloria vaietatis? Contemp. Psychol., 4* (book review), 388–89. *204*

STEVENS, S. S., 1959b. Measurement, psychophysics, and utility. In C. W. Churchman and P. Ratoosh (eds.), *Measurement: definitions and theories,* Ch. 2. New York, Wiley. *205*

STEVENS, S. S., 1960. The psychophysics of sensory functions. *Amer. Sci., 48,* 226–53. *205*

TAJFEL, H., 1957. Value and the perceptual judgment of magnitude. *Psychol. Rev., 64,* 192–204. *75*

TANNENBAUM, P. H., 1956. Initial attitude toward source and concept as factors in attitude change through communication. *Publ. Opin. Quart., 20,* 413–25. *160*

THRASHER, J. D., 1954. Interpersonal relations and gradations of stimulus structure as factors in judgment variations. *Sociometry, 17,* 228–41. *63, 88f.*

THURSTONE, L. L., 1929. Theory of attitude measurement. *Psychol. Rev., 36,* 222–41. *2*

THURSTONE, L. L. and CHAVE, E. J., 1929. *The measurement of attitude.* Chicago, Univ. of Chicago Press. *102, 104, 113*

TRESSELT, MARGARET E., 1947. The influence of amount of practice upon the formation of a scale of judgment. *J. Exper. Psychol., 37,* 251–60. *29, 69, 73*

TRESSELT, MARGARET E., 1948. The effect of the experiences of contrasted groups upon the formation of a new scale of judgment. *J. Soc. Psychol., 27,* 209–16. *73*

TRESSELT, MARGARET E. and VOLKMANN, J., 1942. The production of uniform opinion by non-social stimulation. *J. Abnorm. Soc. Psychol.*, 37, 234–43. *29, 36, 69*

VOLKMANN, J., 1936. The anchoring of absolute scales. *Psychol. Bull.*, 33, 742–43 (abstract). *69*

VOLKMANN, J., 1951. Scales of judgment and their implications for social psychology. In J. H. Rohrer and M. Sherif (eds.), *Social psychology at the crossroads*. New York, Harper. *22, 32ff., 40ff., 181*

VOTH, A. C., 1947. An experimental study of mental patients through the autokinetic phenomenon. *Amer. J. Psychiat.*, 103, 793–805. *34f.*

WAGMAN, M., 1955. Attitude change and authoritarian personality. *J. Psychol.*, 40, 3–24. *159*

WALTER, N., 1955. A study of effects of conflicting suggestions upon judgment of the autokinetic situation. *Sociometry*, 18, 138–46. *34, 66, 79*

WEBB, S. C., 1954. Irregularities in judgment data collected by the method of equal-appearing intervals. *J. Abnorm. Soc. Psychol.*, 49, 415–18. *112, 113*

WEBB, S. C., 1955. Scaling of attitudes by the method of equal-appearing intervals: a review. *J. Soc. Psychol.*, 42, 215–39. *113*

WELLS, F. L., 1907. A statistical study of literary merit, with remarks on some new phases of the method. *Arch. Psychol.*, No. 7. *71*

WEVER, E. G. and ZENER, K. E., 1928. Method of absolute judgment in psychophysics. *Psychol. Rev.*, 35, 466–93. *29, 32f., 36, 69*

WHITE, B. JACK, 1960. The relationship of concept availability to contrast effects in judgment. Doctorate dissertation, Univ. of Oklahoma. *6of.*

WHITTAKER, J. O., 1958. The effects of experimentally introduced anchorages upon judgments in the autokinetic situation. Doctorate dissertation, Univ. of Oklahoma. *34, 64ff.*

WILKE, W. H., 1934. An experimental comparison of the speech, the radio, and the printed page as propaganda devices. *Arch. Psychol.*, No. 169. *147*

WILLIAMS, A. C. and REMMERS, H. H., 1939. Persistence of attitudes concerning conservation issues. *J. Exper. Educat.*, 40, 354–61. *147*

WITKIN, H. A. et al., 1954. *Personality through perception*. New York, Harper, Ch. 1. *21*

WOODROW, H., 1933. Weight-discrimination with a varying standard. *Amer. J. Psychol.*, 45, 391–416. *31, 39f.*

WOODWORTH, R. S. and SCHLOSBERG, H., 1954. *Experimental psychology*. New York, Holt, rev. ed. *20, 25, 31f., 128*

ZELLER, R. C., 1955. Scales of judgment: a determinant of the accuracy of group decision. *Hum. Rel.*, 8, 153–64. *90*

ZIMBARDO, P. G., 1960. Involvement and communication discrepancy as determinants of opinion conformity. *J. Abnorm. Soc. Psychol.*, 60, 86–94. *172f., 197*